Don Harron was born in Toronto and started working in radio and theatre before graduating from the University of Toronto. Since then he has worked in seven plays on Broadway, five in London, and in Shakespeare Festivals in Canada, U.S., and England. He has appeared in several TV series and motion pictures.

Alongside his acting career, Don has been a prolific writer and director. For many years he was closely associated with the annual "Spring Thaw" revue, the 1952 version of which gave birth to the Charlie Farquharson character.

His stage and screen credits include "The Broken Jug" and "The Wonder of It All," and adaptations of "The Adventures of Private Turvey," and the musical "Anne of Green Gables" (winner of the Best Musical Award, 1969-70 season in London).

Charlie Farquharson's Histry of Canada

Don Harron

With an Introduction
by
Max Ferguson

PaperJacks

A division of General Publishing Co. Limited
Don Mills, Ontario

Published in PaperJacks 1976
A division of General Publishing Co., Ltd.
30 Lesmill Rd., Don Mills, Ontario
M3B 2T6

ISBN 0-7737-7118-2
Printed and bound in Canada

1 2 3 4 5 WO 80 79 78 77 76

To the memory of my favourite history teacher, Tommy Tweed

D.H.

Yer Contents

Introduction

I wonder how many of us, gentle readers, smug in the knowl-
edge that during our academic years we had a pretty solid
grounding in Canadian history, can explain why we have two
major railroads running across this country? Be honest now.
Did you really know that it all came about when the two
construction teams — one heading East, the other heading
West — missed each other by a country mile at the rendezvous
point "hard by your Kicking Horse's Ass" and then proceeded on,
laying rail independently until they each reached a coast. I learned
this from Charlie Farquharson as I let him lead me down that
long corridor of quiet time that is Canadian history. It's generally
conceded to be one of the dullest and dreariest walks in the
world, but with Charlie as your guide you just don't want to
come back!

What a wonderful breath of fresh Parry Sound air to blow
away the dust and the cobwebs! It's Charlie's first literary
venture and thank God he hasn't learned the professional's
trick of pacing himself. Charlie comes out of your literary
blocks like a Jesse Owens and goes like Billy Be Damned to
the very end. There's no conserving of energy here — no
niggardly doling out of a *bon mot* maybe every third page to
make creative inspiration last. The sparks of brilliance fly off
every second word and come at you like a salvo out of one of
your average old "rattlin' gat guns."

There's also Valeda — poor long-suffering Valeda — peering
over Charlie's shoulder, all the while hoping that what he has
to say won't get them ridden out of Parry Sound on a rail.
Whenever Charlie gets too outrageous the steadying hand of
Valeda is always there in the form of a "feet note" setting things
straight, counteracting the off-colour Muse that whispers in

Charlie's ear and generally proving that, in Parry Sound at least, your Decency League is more than just a hollow laugh.

But a few things get past Valeda, bless her heart. When Charlie discourses on the Boer War, for example, and Canada's part therein, he informs us that the whole "rang-dang-doo" started because some of your bigger Boors wouldn't let this Englishwoman, Lady Smith, use South Africa's public convéniences. Unlike the Canadian navy, South Africa maintained "apart heads." When Lady Smith finally got herself relieved, however, a lot of our Canadian boys had a hand in it.

Well, Charlie my boy, you've brought off a *tour de force* but I feel I must sound one sobering note. In spite of all your scholarship, in spite of your original style and your refusal to merely ape Gibbon, in spite of aiming higher than Arthur Lower you may be in for a bitter disappointment. I'm afraid it's a foreskin concussion that all the accolades will go to a fella by the name of Darn Herring. I don't see how it can be avoided. Life's like that, Charlie, you do all the work and somebody else gets the credit!

Max Ferguson

Yer Fore-Word

Well sir, Billy, I s'pose you'd like to know how Charlie Farquharson come to be all of a sudden one day historical.

I mind it was last spring. I was out with the tractor jist this side of my hardwood bush. I'd finished up the spring ploughin' so I was havin' kind of a harrowin' day. It's not too bad when you plough her, but my gol when yer on the harrows you have to stop all the time fer to git them big stones outen the way.

Well sir, I'd jist gotten offa my Allis Chalmers . . . that's the name of my tractor fer you city folks . . . and was jist startin' to pry a fair-size piece of granite outen the path of the harrows, when I seen this fella leanin' fernenst the fence. He was there watchin' me heave my stones.

Now you take yer av'rage stranger leanin' fernenst a fence and that's all he's doin', means one of two things: either he's one of yer unemployables or he's workin' fer the guvermint.

Turns out this fella's a genial-ologist workin' fer the Department of Mind yer Resources. He was goin' 'round the country collectin' samples of rock. That's all he was doin', and gittin' paid fer it too. And he was jist waitin' till I got offa my tractor before he asked me if I minded him gittin' his rocks offa my farm.

"My gol," I said, "you can jist folley along in front of the harrows and take all of 'em. But what in the Sam Hill do you want with all that rock anyways?"

And do you know what this sibilant servant told me? He told me that the rocks hard by my hardwood bush was over two billion five hundert million year old. Now I know them guvermint fellas is fond of yer inflation, but my gol, even if you cut her in haff, that's still old.

He called my stones by a funny name too. Now you take yer av'rage rock on the farm, I'd purty well allus taken 'em fer granite. But this fella says, take away yer top soil and when you git right

1

down to it, the Farquharson farm is just a lotta schist. That's what she's called, yer pre-Cambrian schist, what was dropped off by them glacy-ears jist after yer last Ice Age.

Now when I say yer last Ice Age I'm not talkin' 'bout yer Winter of '71 when we had twelve foot of snow. If yer gonna look at this thing real historical yer gonna have to go way back beyond yer behind of that.

'Sides, I don't wanta say too much about yer winter here in Canada. I figger if you don't say too much mebbe it'll go away like it did once between Ice Ages and ev'rythin' got cam and bammy fer a time. Yer climate is a main factor of yer histry, and most of Canada is even today out doors. And that makes fer an offal lotta hoppin', jumpin', and runnin' about jist to keep warm, 'stead of gittin' down to bizness. I figger the hole histry of our country woulda bin differnt if yer temperchure had bin razed jist a few degrees of Fornheat. You take yer av'rage temperchure even today, it's purty mean.

Anyways, if yer ready, put yer feet in the stove and we'll git started with my oriole histry of Canada . . . that jist means it was took down by the wife Valeda, writin' fast as Billy-yo jist as it come outta my mouth. I woulda writ it down myself, but Valeda says nobody's gonna read writin' when it's written rotten. Seems there's two kinds of histry, yer oriole and yer annual, but I ain't got the time to do this ev'ry year.

Yer Universal

Histry is somethin' you can't never finish, so you might jist as well git it started at the beginnin'.

I guess Adam and Eve is about the oney ones what really know how the hole thing git started. I'm talkin' 'bout yer Earth when she was jist settin' out . . . oh . . . musta bin neons ago.

Of course yer Earth, she's jist part of yer Universal. That's the hole rang-dang-doo rolled into one — yer Spiro Nebulous, yer assteroids, yer Big Dippy, and the rest of yer heavenly constellapations.

Now even the scientificks and assterologists don't seem to agree on how this hole rig got a shove fer to git it started. There's some as says yer Universal never got begun at all. They say she's allus bin there in yer solid state, and it's there she's goin' to stay through yer light years and yer dark.

On the other hands, there's some scientificks as says the hole thing started with a ring-tailed snorter of a spondiferous decombustin'. In other words, things got off to a Big Bang and the intire proceedin's bin goin' downhill ever since.

Now there you have yer two differnt theces to play with. You can b'leeve in yer solid state if you like, but the wife and myself is kinda parshul to yer Big Bang.

Yer Old Mother Earth

Now way back, mebbe a million skillion years B.C. (that'd be Before Confederation) there was nothin' much hangin' up in the sky but yer Sun. I don't even think yer Moon was workin' at that time. Jist a twenty-four hour day fulla Sun, like they git up Furbisher Bay way come Dumbminion Day.

Well sir, there's some as holds, and in books too, that our Earthly body was really jist a cooled-down bit of gas let off from yer Sun. Isn't that a ring-tailed snorter of a thought fer the day?

There was yer Sun, mindin' his own bizness, jist doin' his orebit while crossin' the circum-interference of yer Universal, when all of a sudden he let go a belch and there we was.**

Well sir, after things got cooled down a bit, give or take a coupla millenemas later, that little burp got a bit of a crust on her, what they call yer molson lava. And by and by, by gol, if the rest of that gas din't evaporize into water. So that was it, yer water and yer molson lava with a little muddy dirt to keep things together. Not much of a start, but that'd be what come to be yer Old Mother Earth.

But that's, of course, if you folley yer Big Bang. If you side with them other Solid Staters, then you got ev'ry right in this world to say our Earth come from nothin', and is headed in the same direction.

** Soler Feetnote: Yer heartburn at the surface of yer solar's plexus has got to be close to a coupla thousand degrees Fornheat. No wonder we was got rid of.

4

Yer Ups and Yer Downs

Well now, after yer Mother Earth got seprate from yer Sun and got left outside to cool, she started to set after a spell. That was when yer molson lava went all hard and become what they call yer ignorous and fatuous rocks.

And the crustier old Mother Earth got, the more she started to wrinkle and fold up fast. All the big rocks got together and started to pull themselves up into mountain chains. The little stones, them as couldn't swing the chain, they had to slink down, dis-intergrate to gravel, and become valleys, 'cause there had to be somethin' between them mountains.**

Mind you, the mountains what sprung up, they're not the ones you see today when you go to Lake Louise to Banf (whatever that is?).*** Nosirree, Bob, the first mountains has all since come unsprung and has been ground down to a stump, jist like yer av'rage married man.

You take yer Rockies, they is jist upstarts comparisoned to all that worn-down schist 'round my place. You see, the Farquharson farm is right in the middle of what they now call yer Great Canadian Shield. (My gol, it's all I can do to recognize the new flag and sing the first few lines of "O Canada" without worryin' about a Shield, too.)

I b'leeve they call it yer Great Canadian Shield 'cause fer years it's bin lyin' there flat and takin' whatever comes to her . . . givin' up her minerals and water without too much of a struggle.

** Cosmickal Feetnote: This was all done accordion to yer Laws of Gravelty which somebody passed away back even then.

*** Rocky Feetnote: My boy Orville can frug (whatever that is) but he don't know how to Banf.

Yer Plastocine Period

Now don't git me wrong. The hole she-bang hadn't cooled down all that much from yer molson state. Jist 'cause some of the pushyer rocks become permoted to mountains don't mean they wasn't havin' a hot time down in the valleys alone. I mean they wasn't still on the bubble or nothin'; but neither was they what you'd call yer good temperate. I don't exactly recall my zone at the time, but I'd say that the Parry Sound-Muskoka district back then was purty sub-topical, with weather all year 'round like we have fer the thrashin'.

It's what they call yer Plastocine Period 'cause under them rocks it was still a bit gummy and gooey. Why if you lived up Parry Sound way in them days you wouldn'ta needed to git to Florida atall. Yer North Bay and yer Flim Flam and even yer Yella-knife they was all part of a steam-heated jungle. No firs at all. Jist pam trees camly swayin' in the sweaty breeze.

And the things what come out from under them rocks! Great big riptiles thirty-forty feet high, they coulda picked lunch outen the top of yer silo. You woulda had to stand up on the stool to milk 'em, these Dinashores and Brontesores. They was mostly Vegetary-aryans. All they was after was them tender leaves at the top of the tree, like it says in the tea-bag advertizin'.

Of course, accordin' to yer Theery of yer Revolution, which depends upon the survival of yer fitness, there had to be somethin' around to spoil yer Dinashores fun. And that'd be a fierce lookin' dragoon with teeth like a hay-rake, called yer Tronto-soreass Wrecks. It was his job to make all the rest of them ex-stink. Him not bein' a Vegetary-aryan he hung around them others mainly because of the meat.

But even yer Tronto-soreass got ex-stinked when the heat got turned off, the Ice Age come on, and all that meat got put into the deep freeze.

Yer Terrain Drain

Ev'rybody's yappin' nowadays 'bout them Yanks grabbin' at our assets. But I can't figger what them U.S.es is after they hasn't already got down there in that Land of yer Free and Easy.

Even back durin' yer first Ice Age, they got the pick of our topsoil. You take them big glacy-ears movin' down from Furbisher Bay and puttin' us all in cold storage; well, all that icin' pushed the cream of our loam in front of it and dumped it over yer Forty-ninth parallel of lassitude.**

So now we're down to yer rock-bottom, and all that creamy loam is part of yer Great American Dessert. And it's still oozin' down that way every time there's a spring run-off. There's no need for them Yanks to come up here and cut our water off. The Law of Gravelty has been in affect in both countries and all they have to do is wait. You look at yer globe and you can watch our country run downhill. Ever since time in memorial we bin tricklin' down to the States.

Now that all happen after our ten thousand year cold snap, when somebody changed yer thermos-stat, and Canada become yer meltin' plot. Now, mind, it never got back to bein' yer topical rain forest.*** But things did start to warm up with a few prevailin' Westerlies from Killalloo and a coupla Shnooks from Caligary.

Mind you, jist when things was gittin' nice, back down would come yer wall of ice puttin' the freeze back on yer plants, yer crops, yer livestock, and yer wages and prices. This here re-occurrants happen three or four times, and all that shiftin' ice kinda disencouraged steady settlement, so fer quite a spell Canada got more or less uninhibited.

** Split Feetnote: Better known as yer Great Devide.

*** Wet Feetnote: 'Cept mebbe fer Vancoover.

Yer Pre-Historic Man

Gol darnit, it's time to git offa the land and onto yer lively stock. I guess ev'rybody knows that we never coulda begun standin' on our hind legs with our thumbs up in the air.

I b'leeve it was hard onto four-score and seven thousand year ago our fore-paws walked upon this earth.** Before man was Man, he was jist another Mammyal***, and fer quite some time he felt purty much like a fish . . . outta water.

Let's face it, yer old-time man warn't too differnt from the rest of yer apish gibberons, orange-utangs, and bassoons. I mean you put 'em all together and none of 'em stuck out much. They was all pretty hairy and walkin' low to the ground on all floors. And they all of 'em lived by yer Law of the Jungle — Let Us Prey (still inforce today).

But the main differnce 'tween yer monkey incesters and yer Prime-evil man was yer tool. You take yer av'rage mammyal, they wasn't too much on brains altho' offal high on the in-stinks. But durin' yer gorilla warfare, yer early man had enough scents to pick somethin' up offa the ground and bash the other prime mates brains around with it. And all that brain-bashin' was the start of yer civilly-eyezation.

** Fore-Feetnote: And if we'd never had got up offa them, we might be better off in yer lumber regions today, accordin' to yer Osterpaths and Cairo-practicers.

*** Teat Note: Yer Mammyal was so called 'cause he'd breast feed 'stead of suckin' eggs, and was all the time yellin' fer his Mammy.

Yer Earlier Inhibitants

Yer Royl Ontaryo Mosuleum says the real name of yer Prime Evil man was, git this, Pithy-can-throw-puss Erecter. Valeda din't want me to find out what that meant. She was jist releeved to find out there wasn't no such rough-neck hangin' 'round our parts when Canada got populous.

In fack, there's no such thing as yer Old Canadian. I don't care what yer Benighted Umpire Roylists says, yer first new Canadians was jist a buncha forn immigrance. And so has ev'ry one of us since bin, if you want to look at it from a genial-logical point of you.

I bet them blue bleeders on yer Socialist Register will be madder'n Billy-yo when they find out the first famblies of Canada come from somewheres in Utter Mongolia hard by yer Go-by Dessert. They probly slipped thru a coupla chinks in yer Great Wall one day, got lost, and ended up in our backyard after they got their berings strait.

Now them as could stand the cold settled right down in yer Artick, started chippin' away at them glacy-ears till they cut themselves up an iglue, and started havin' a whale of a time livin' offa the ice.

But the rest of them Orientails as din't take to joinin' yer Polar Bare Club, left them friggid platitudes and hightailed it south fer to spend winter, summer, fall, spring, and anythin' else they could lay their hands on.

Now how did a buncha tourist coulees become all of a sudden yer av'rage Injians? Well sir, surprise, surprise, if they din't meet up with another buncha forners was come up from yer deep south. I don't mean yer early Victorians from the Vancoover Island. I mean yer deep, deep south of the border like where yer Argenteeny grouchos comes from.

Now don't ask me why them Spanish senior-eaters come up here. Most likely to forge fer their stock since it was them fly-by-knights first brung yer horse up here, and our prayery jist seemed to be their oyster.

Well, of course, when yer China-man met up with yer Mexa-calley Rose things jist natcherly started to happen. But Valeda don't b'leeve that sorta stuff belongs in a histry book.**

So if you still don't know where we all of us come from, git yer big brother to tell you, or better still, keep yer eyes open 'round the barnyard.

** Orville Feetnote: 'Specially now that our boy Orville is gittin' inner-ested in kissin' girls, ever since last summer when he got his tongue stuck in a coke bottle.

Yer tipical Injian smokin' and dryin' moose meat

Yer Nobel Savitch

That's what they're callin' yer av'rage Injian. Not too long ago they was referred to as drunken welfarers who wasn't fit to be let in yer local dance, and this year they's all of a sudden parrygones of virchew. Nobody seems to want to let them be jist what they are . . . represt human beans the Guvermint has reservations about.

Now you take yer av'rage Injian, there aren't no such thing. I mean yer West Coaster is in a differnt kettle of fish from yer Marrytimer. They wouldn'ta known what each other was even talkin' about (jist like today in yer Untidy Nations).

Take yer B.C. tribes, they was out spawnin' offa yer salmon in their two-cedar canews (them was yer compacks) and the big fellas, yer four-cedars, was made from Duglass firs and was called dug-outs ('cept fer lunch when they become cook-outs, and them Injians'd porridge right in their canew).

Then all them Coaster tribes, yer Hyeedas, yer Quackyoodles, and yer Squeamish'd head back home to their token poles and them big-beamed houses bilt jist like their women.

Now yer Plain Injian, him with all the feathers up his bonnet, he'd never seen a tin of salmon. He lived on and offa his horse, and as long as he was knee-deep in buffalo they was in the chips. Mrs. Plain Injian she'd do down a lotta buffalo fer the winter and put them up in pemmycans. Then they'd pack up their wampum, put the caboose on their back, and be off somewheres else acrost yer Nomad's land.

One of them Stampeed tribes, yer Stoneys, they learnt how to make fire with a few little chippies and a fire-drill and everythin' would go up in smoke from all that science friction. After that they found some loco weed to put in their stoned pipes and passed them around after a piece, till ev'rybody got to laughin' and snick-

13

erin' and they couldn't be bothered with any more huntin' and fatherin'.**

Today them Plain Injians is left with next to nothin'. Jist a stoney stare, discouragin' words, and not a buffalo heard in site.

Now yer squattin' and sowin' Injians was yer farmers from Ontary-ario and Cuebec — yer Allgonkyouwin, yer Eeryquoit, and yer Ureon. Mind you it was the woman-folk, what they call yer squash, what done most of yer fieldwork. The fellas was off chasin' yer fur-borin' animals on snowshoes.***

Come thrashin' time, it was yer squash what hode and harvested yer maze (corn to us). The men they'd jist hang around the lodge and raise hell after strainin' their corns, which they called yer Great Spirit.

Yer Cuebec Injians they was mostly out in yer forest workin' as yer birch bark strippers. They din't wear no fancy feathers on *their* Eastern bonnets, 'cause they might've gotten tangled in their under-brush. After a hard day's strippin' tho', they'd more'n likely put on a lotta make-up and go to their lodge meetin' and dance with each other. Takes all kinds, don't it!

Now yer Marrytime Injians, yer Mixmax, they got the shorty end of yer stick as usual and life fer them was mostly dulse. But purty soon the white man was comin' to bring them all the comforts of civilly-eyezation: axes, knives, guns, smallpox, measles and tuber colossus, to say nothin' 'bout yer demon-rarer rum.

***

** Wrong Feetnote: This here's a typathetickle era. It was huntin' and gatherin' they din't feel like, 'cept fer more loco weed, which I suspeck was first cuzzin to yer marryjewanna, or yer Hishash, or yer L.C.D.

*** Funny Feetnote: Don't ask me where them animals got them snow-shoes. I jist copied that detale strait down from the histry book.

—

14

Yer Norse Sagass

So far as yer Yerup, yer Azure, and yer Africker in them old-time times, Canada was purty much on yer Continental Shelf. Nobody in yer forn parts knew or cared much who or where our place was. That hasn't changed all that much, I guess.

The first fellas to sneak away for a weekend in our outports was yer Viking. They was big blond sailors from the Scandalnavya with horny hats. Of course nobody would ever a-heard 'bout them sneakin' in and out if it hadn't bin fer yer Sagass — turble long pomes that gives you some idee of what's really behind a Norse's tale.

Now yer Norse they was in the plunderin', pillagin', harryin', and layin' waste bizness. Sometimes they burnt people's houses over their head, but that's where the rent had got to anyways, and nobody din't seem to mind all that much, since they was purty busy bein' pillaged and harried.

Them Norse was hangin' 'round Iceland (not to be confused with a skatin' rink of the same name in Port Carlin') when they decided to see how far they could get on one galleon. They got as far as yer Greenland, which is darn good mileage. If they'da brung a furmometer with 'em, they'da never called it Greenland . . . more like Blueland, it was cold enuff to freeze the knots offa blue spruce.

Yer locals was a buncha Eskymo. Now there's not too much you can plunder and pillage from yer av'rage Eskymo but a mess of blubber. My gol, did you ever try burnin' an iglue over anybody's head? So them Vikings jist settled down fer the winter and laid waist.

The cheef of them Norses, Eric yer Red . . . one of the Roosian branch of the family . . . finely give up yer Greenland acres and went down the coast as far as Road Island, where I b'leeve he still has some family (you probly heard of yer Road Island Reds).

His son, Leaf yer Lucky, he stuck it out, foolin' 'round yer

Labbydoor and yer Hallyfacks on weekends hopin' to live up to his name. Finely he ended up in James Bay without so much as a projeck, so he hit fer the States and finely ended up in Minnyapples where he become yer first Norse Amerken. He later died and become known as Leaf yer Lucky Stiff.

A lotta people wonder why none of them Vikings ever staid in Canada. My gol, why should they be any differnt from ev'rybody else?

Yer Godfather of Our Country

You take yer av'rage Eyetaliân they's jist one big family, what they call yer Cosy Nostril. It's so intermate they're allus huggin' and kissin' each other to death in public.

Things was no differnt then. Even yer Middle Age ones stuck together even tho' they was wanderin' all over the earth. You take yer Mark O'Polo, from the canals of Venus. He was a travellin' salesman got as far as Peeking and brung back some spicy stories.

He musta told them to Chris Clumbuss, 'cause he right away took four girls with him on a Carrybean cruise — Nina, Pinta, Sandy, and Maria. I don't know what he uncovered about them, mind, but ev'ry school kid knows what else he was lookin' fer, when "Clumbuss sailed the ocean blue in nineteen hundert and forty-two."**

But them 'Merkens got nothin' on us. We was found by our own Eyetalian! Do you mind John Cabot? Sounds like he come from Boston, but he was another one of them Marrytime MafiasCo. Since he was workin' fer the Anglish King, Henry Seven***, they made him change his name to somethin' they could pernounce 'stead of somethin' you might find on a meatball menyou.

Now, King Henry sent our John to look fer a root to the Far East, and Cabot's trail led from the port of Bristle strait to Newfieland. So he done what the King told him, 'cause, by gol, if St. John's ain't yer Far East I don't know what is.

He brung along his son, Sebastian Cabot, too, makin' it a family affair. Sebastian he was in the reg'lar bizness of takin' credit fer his father's acheevments, and he done so good at it he retired even

** Corrective Feetnote: It was actually 1492. Jist ignore that bit of misinflammation.

*** Royl Feetnote: Henry Seven, he wasn't the fella had the six wives, Anne Balloon, Jane Arden and all them others and later died of gunner-rear. That was next year's model, Henry Eight.

before his father got pensioned off. Which was oney ten pounds a year after King Henry found out his tame Eyetalian had discovered Newfieland 'stead of Sam Arcand and Ind. Them Anglish figgered that this mistake was a wopper. Which is too bad, gol darnit, 'cause yer St. John's is a purty darn good port in any storm. And ice free too.** It's too bad Henry din't b'leeve in cod.

** Cold Feetnote: Ice free. Drinks fifty cents. Open Sundys too.

Yer Godfather of Our Country discoverin' yer Far East

Yer Porchygeese

It's more 'n likely that much of yer Newfieland wasn't all that much new found. Now there's a place called Porchygull jist this side of yer Spain town line, and their fishermen'd bin hangin' 'round our Marrytimes fer a cod's age, smeltin' fer deposits in yer Grand Banks.

Now you take yer av'rage fisherman, he don't mind talkin' 'bout yer fish what got away, but he's not gonna tell anyone where he gets 'em if he does. When it comes to that, he's no loose lipper; he'll clam up like yer small-mouthed bass.

So who's to say that them Porchygeese wasn't fishin' 'round our place long before yer Clumbuss and yer Cabot, but they jist had the good cents to shut up 'bout this nice quiet spot they found to drop their hook. They never writ up them sorta things. Why a coupla them fellas, Madge-ellen and Fiasco de Gamba, even circum-ambulated yer globe without none of us in Parry Sound hearin' 'bout it in none of our scool books. Our books was too busy makin' a fuss 'bout the bowls of Sir Francis D. Rake and Sir Walter Rally, him as kept yer Virgin Queen spotless.

And there was the odd Porchygoose or Spainyard goin' 'round yer Horn by way of yer A-sores. One of yer Main Spanish, stout Kortex, was too fat to git 'round yer Horn, so he stuck around yer Issmus of Pananama and figgered the easy way to work up yer passage to yer Far East was to check yer zone laws and bild a canal. Don't know why nobody'd seen that before, yer canal root. Seems alimentary to me.

So this rang-dang-doo 'bout who foundered what and when is probly by now become a-crocker. As Valeda says, after we git offa the party-line, "Nobody ever tells us anythin'."

Yer Great Breton, Jack Carter*

I b'leeve I shoulda mentioned before that there's another kinda Injians 'sides yer red fellas. I'm talkin' 'bout them holy rollers on the banks of yer Gangrene River wearin' nothin' but a diaper and a durban wrapped around theirselves while they practice yer yoghurt sittin' on a bed of four-inch nails. I don't know how them Injian Swanees can sit on them C.P.R. spikes and not feel a thing, but Valeda says it must be like bein' married fer thirty years.

Anyways, them Injians was the abie-originals that Clumbuss was lookin' fer when he all of an accidental uncovered Amerka. Din't matter that he met a lotta bare-naked locals wearin' feathers and mocksins and jay-cloths on their loins 'stead of yer wrap-me-round nappykins, he figgered he'd ended up in that other Injia.** Maybe Clumbuss figgered that they was shellin' out fer Hallyween with all that wore paint on their cheeks and macnamara on their eyebrows.

Anyways, the nackname he give them sure stuck. And so did the idee of gittin' to Bumbay or Calcutter by way of yer Hallyfacks and Cuebec City. That was the bug in yer bonnet of yer next famousexplorer.***

I b'leeve she'd be about 15:34 Eastern Standard when Jack Carter set sail from the Port of St. O'Malley lookin' fer the wealth of Far Camay. Now you'd think anybody with any cents'd head strait fer yer Medium-terranian or even yer Cake of Good Hoke,

* Other Feetnote: Pernounced Jock Carshay if yer by-lingamal.

** Wanderin' Feetnote: Valeda says you should always cheque yer tickets.

*** Tight Feetnote: Valeda's sorry she got them two jammied together. Yer Jack Carter he wasn't no famous-sexplorer; he was jist lookin' fer a piece of land.

22

but thanks to them Porchygeese and their wild tails, Jack Carter he lit out strait fer yer Newfie Happy Fishin' Grounds too.

I don't know what he expected to find goin' thru yer Straights of Belial, but he finely dropped his anker in Shallure Bay, which is French fer bein' in hot water. It sure musta bin a warm summer, 'cause the next place he dropped his anker he called yer Gasp Bay. I don't mind he ever found that anker agin, but he wound up down yer St. Lorrent waterway still lookin' fer them Himmel-upalaya Mountings.

All he did find was a buncha wig-warms at Cuebec City run by a Injian chiefess, Donna Coma. She was in charge of yer Red Feather campains fer her tribe. Cuebec City, by the way, was called Static Coma after her father who had become post-mortis and gone up to the Happy Hauntin' Grounds. Donna she later hit the big time in the States when she changed her name to Pokey Hauntus, but there was a roomer she also registered as Mrs. John Smith.

Now at that time Jack Carter he was lookin' fer the gold of yer Taj Maher but Canada was still on yer fur standard. All Donna Coma had was a buncha pup tents but the grass was dry and they had a good time anyways. And when Jack asked Donna to show him the Seven Wonders 'Round yer World, she said she'd take him to the Mount Royal fer the weekend.**

Donna Coma taut Jack to paddle her stern in a canew too, and they got all the way up to the fork of yer Ottawa where she had some more relations. Jack he wanted to go further up with her, sort of Ganaknockyou way, but he warn't that good in a canew and couldn't pass his rabbids test.

** Candlesteined Feetnote: Not yer hotel, which wasn't yet, but to the top of the hill what's named after the old Garlic word fer Montreal.

But Donna did manage to interjuice him to the old Injian sport of Lacrotch which he took back to France and has since become yer national's past-time. He brung somethin' else back to France too. It says in them histry books it was a big case of Scurfy, one of the poplar maladys of the day. Anyway that's what they say it was, and that's good enough fer my wife Valeda. She don't hold with none of yer sociable diseases.

"Jimmy sweeze apple Jock Carshay."

(By-lingamal replay: "Hi! My name's Jack Carter, can I squeeze your apples?")

Yer Pole's Passage

I guess the main reason yer av'rage Canadian has been infeerier in his complecks is the fack that nobody ever really wanted to visit us in the first place. Them exploiters was all lookin' fer the gold and spicys of yer Tartery and yer Southeast Azure. Now why anybody would go further north and west fer to git south and east, don't make no cents. 'Cept to yer Anglish mebbe.**

Them Anglish never wanted Canada. To them it was somethin' to by-pass around like yer prostrate gland. The first few times they tried it they kept bumpin' into yer Labbydoor. So bein' ex-scentrick they went further north, figgerin' on runnin' up around yer Pole fer to git to yer topical places with the hot climacks. You take yer av'rage Anglishman he'll allus do it the hard way, like standin' up in a hammock. Mind you they're a pretty friggid bunch anyways, havin' not bin in central heat since the Roamins was in their gloamin' 'bout 55 B.B.C.

Mind you they did try runnin' North-east first-off, but they kept hittin' yer Serviett Roosia. They even got as far as yer Crumlin where they done some tradin' with yer Muskyvites and set up an east end branch of yer Hudson Bayco, called yer Muskovary Company.***

But there was a lotta crazy Angled-Sacksons up in our Artick at the same time — Humpy Filbert, Marty Furbisher, and Look Focks — but the jimmy dido what become a big name was Henry Hudson, who has since become a bay, a river, a departmental store, and a car that's now obsolene.

Now Henry he went far. He got past yer Bafflin Island and yer

** Stubbern Feetnote: Tippical bull-head people, yer Anglish, says Valeda who's mostly Scotch but still won't touch it.

*** Red Feetnote: Valeda says it don't sound like fit company, and besides it don't pay to git too meaty with yer Reds, some of 'em is Commonists.

Straights of Umgawa till he got into that big dead end which was his namesake by posterior. Mind you, Hudson's Bay had no company yet and yer Moose Factory wasn't turnin' out moose, and the crew wanted to git to where there was somethin' to do on shore leave like Goose Bays. But Henry he drug them all down to the James Bay hard by yer Timmins and Cockran, and tole 'em he planned to winter it out till fly-time fishin' thru the ice. Well the crew wanted to spend their winter in a Corner Brook bar fishin' thru the ice fer palomino cherries. They up and held a mutininny and was gonna make Henry and his son Orville walk yer divin' board, but it was so cold they woulda broke their necks on the ice, so the crew jist left them with abandon.

Now if you look up yer histry directomies, they'll try and tell you nobody don't know what happen to Henry and the little Hudson. But my gol, lookit yer map hard by New Jersey. It's sure oblivious to me that Henry left the ice bizness and went into yer down-river trade where he finely come out down there jist this side of yer Statute of Libertations. He may of bin the first, but he sure warn't the last of us to retire and head south. Jist like that Eepy Tailor and Casey Irving that has the nerve to sit on their holdin's and sing "Yes, We Have No Bahamas."

In Yer Hat

There was allus somethin' fishy 'bout the start of yer Canada, with all them Porchygeese net-minders draggin' theirselves around, and even the Spanish fly-casting all over the place. It was gittin' so crowded with forners 'bout this time, yer Grand Banks started to close at three o'clock.

In fack, Newfieland purty near become one of yer Spanish Might 'n Main possessions till one of them Anglish free-booties, Sir Humpy Filbert, come bargin' into St. John's, jumped their ships, stuck his nose in their focussles, and snatched the catch in yer Spainyard's hatch. This he done all in the good name of Queen Bessie, which used to be virgin till it was lost in the mists of her time.

Now if any of them forners had done the same thing to us, we woulda beat about their bush callin' them all sortsa things. We'd a figgered them fer plain pierats and probly give them a whiff of grape-nuts on their broadside. But since we done it ourselves, us Angled-Sacksons genally call it yer explore-atory research 'stead of what it really is — jist another buck-an-ear wavin' his skull and crotchbones.

But them Bask fishymen was tired anyways of exposin' theirselves to our wind and weather, and they was longin' to head fer home as soon as they dried their cod-pieces. Seems nobody ever wanted to hang around our place till somebody found out there was money to be made in the hat bizness.

Yes sir, leave it to beaver fer to settle up Canada. This dam animal is really the Mother of Our Country on accounta the hair on its back bein' so desecrative that purty soon all yer high mucky-mucks and sassiety people wanted to git felt.

Now you've heard of yer Paris hat. The wife she bought one once when she was had by cuzzins down to Brantford. Well, it was them

French city Parisites before ev'rybody else is allus incrusted with what's *a la mode*. And yer beaver soon become Number One on yer Hat Parade. Seems strange to have a whole country git settled up jist from what that poemicist Rudeyard Kippalong used to call "a hanka hair and a piece a tail."

Yer Pork Royl

I guess one of yer most poplar games in the old-time France would be Monopply. The rools was set by yer French King-pin Henry Four (not to be confused with yer Birtish King Henry Four, what was sub-divisioned by Shakespeer into two parts).

Now 'sides yer usual Monopply rools (Do Not Pass Go, Go Dreckly To Jail) yer French rooler he figgered the oney way to play the game was to corner yer beaver market and make them traders and trappers stay there thru the winter fer immigrance, 'cause if you keep yer trap shut all winter you miss a lotta fur pieces. Henry figgered in the summertime them trappers could take to farmin' since farmin' is considered by most of yer Middle-Aged Kings to be the backbone of yer hole civilly-eyezation. And I s'pose they was right, give or take a coupla inches.

Anyways, yer first settlement was bilt in a ring 'round yer Analappolis Basin and called yer Pork Royl. That was on accounta the King sent along a coupla tons of fat-back fer to last them thru till mebbe yer twenty-fourth of May. Well sir, by the time that day come 'round, ev'rybody was sick of pork and nobody was speakin' to one another, they was so salty.

Too bad, 'cause when they started out some of the times they had had was good. 'Specially when they all took orders fer yer Good Cheer, a kinda after-hours club set up by their Good Cheerleader, yer Seer de Months, to keep all their spirits flowin' reg'lar. His work was later carried on somethin' fierce in Montreal by yer Seer de Molson who brung on yer Golden Aged.

Marg Lescargot, one of yer Good Cheerios, she got up a concert called yer Theatre of Neptoon, which keeps on till this day hard by

Hallyfacks and musta bin purty near the first of yer Minion Drama Festerall.**

Anyways, come fly-time all them Pork Roylers was ready to pack up their charter and take flight back home. I guess mebbe they'd had enough of yer capitalist's punishment, 'cause they jist said "The hell with Novy Scotia, let yer dark and dreary mountings be . . ." (which was later made famous by the wife's favourite mezzanine soprano, Kathleen McCinnamon, the one who's claimed to have the voice of an Angle).

You can still see the ring them Pork Roylers left 'round the Basin, but that Analappolis never got settled down fer another twenty year, when yer Scotch was moved in and gave proof to the locals they had the stuff to last. About ninety proof.

** Sore Feetnote: The wife she thinks that hole D.D.F. thing is a fake. Valeda got all the way to elimination in yer Northern Ontaryo semi-finals year before last takin' off the part of one of yer "Private Wives" by Nold Cowherd, and she never got so much as a dishonourable mention.

Takin' orders fer yer Good Cheer at Pork Royl

Yer Founderer

Not all of them Royl Porkers went back to France. One of the biggest stayed behinds was yer cardiographer** of the outfit who had his heart set on applyin' fer permanent resonance.

This fella's full monicker'd be Samuel D. Shamplain, but he musta sent a lotta wires acrost yer Atalantic, 'cause he's genally known by his short form, jist Sam Plain.

Whatever his name, he's known as yer Founderer of Cuebec, the fella what stayed behind and stuck to his guns, then traded them to the Injians fer furs. Sam done so well with the gun-runnin' that them Allgonkyouwin Injians kept pelting him with beaver. They invited him to a party with some Eeryquoits from New York, 'cept it turned out to be a war party and Sam showed off with his old repeater. I guess the first bang an Injian gang ever heard was fired by Sam, which din't please them Eeryquoits too much on accounta Sam was shootin' at them.

He dropped mebbe one little, two little, three little Eeryquoits and the rest of them hitched up their feathers and high-tailed it back to their New York stompin' grounds hard by yer Manhatin Island. But don't ask me why all them New Yorkers had got in Dutch when them Neitherlanders took over and called it New Hamstersdam. The Injians got along good with their Dutch Masters who stood them to drinks which was quite a treat considerin' yer Manhatin cost at the time twenty four dollars. Shows you that big city prices suffered from inflammation even then.

But between Sam Plain and them Old Dutch Gleaners, they sure brung up the Redman's standard of dyin'. Not fergettin' yer small

---

** Scaley Feetnote: That's a fancy handle fer mapsmaker, mapsmaker make me a map, like the old song goes from Fiddlin' Around Up On yer Roof.

35

pox which didn't take long to grow into a full-pledged epidermic and become yer big pox on both their houses.

Mind you, Sam Plain interjuiced some good things too. He riz up the first high-rise in down-town Static Coma (Cuebec to you). It was a superiory complecks called yer Habit-tot on accounta they even took in couples with child.

But one child they disallowed in there was Mrs. Sam Plain who was oney a twelve-years-old miner when they was married. Now twelve in them days was sooner than yer "age of intent" and so fer quite a time she had to stay in France, bein' kept outta Cuebec by their well-known Padlock Law.

Now Sam felt this law was a frustrate thing to keep him from comin' to be yer Father of New French. He was so cheesied off that when some more Anglish free-booties dropped their ankers on Cuebec, Sam left the hole thing to them and went back to Paris on yer passionate leave.

But he come back in a coupla years after them Anglish got free-booted out, and this time he brung his teeny-age wife with him, but he was smart enuff to include along one of them Jesyouwait priests as baby-sitter.

I dunno whether married life agreed with Sam or no, but it was about this time he started leavin' his Habit-tot a lot and spendin' summers with the boys up on Georgian Bay. First he went up river on the Ottawa and tried to paddle past the site of yer Common House but was turned back by a great wind.

The wife she claims Sam Plain musta stopped by Parry Sound one day fer lunch 'cause she found a small momento of his a few years back on the fourth concession down by the town line. It had an old rusty knob fallin' to pieces, and when she took it to our Town Librarium fer to find out what it was, he told her Sam Plain musta used it fer a sextant. Valeda's never bin back to that Liberry since.

36

Sam Plain takin' a peek at his sextant

Yer Man on His Terre

Cuebec City got kinda quiet when Sam and his Plainsmen was busy-tourin' 'round the stix, so them as stayed behind thought they should think up another place it would be fun to go on a weekend.

The fella what really thunk it up, his name was yer Seer de Masonsnerves. The King sent him out with some of his palisades fer to bild this place, Ville Marie, outta wood logs and fur posts. Jist the thing fer to catch yer curiest tooriest.

Masonsnerves he was allus a big booster fer to git visitors fer to come and see his mountin. He'd be like that Jean Dropout, who's now carryin' the torch fer yer Olymphian Games despite his Exposé in '67.

Now mind you, it took quite a time fer Montreal to become what it is today, yer modren Sodomy Begorrah. That Jesyouwait priest brung over by Sam Plain got all his R.C. friends to come. So many of them in fack that it was hard to keep up with the holy orders.

I figger about this time there was as many habits and hassocks as there was reg'lar inn-habitants. Seems ev'rybody all of a sudden got the old time religion. Even down in them Boston States they got landed with a buncha Puritanicals from Angland. They got offa that S.S. Maytag, gathered up a lotta Plymouth Rocks, and settled down to lay their own settlement.

Now you'd think them Anglican Londoners and yer R.C. Parishioners would git along jist fine, and probly organize a taffy pull after the Bingo. And they woulda too if they'd stuck to farmin', 'cause come thrashin' time ev'rybody helps ev'rybody else no matter how hard you can't stand 'em. 'Sides, ev'rybody loves ev'rybody after six differnt pieces of pie.

But in them days they was still havin' a fur-fer-all. With all them expensive coats runnin' 'round on four legs nobody had a mind to be hoein' and hayin' and geein' and hawin'. They knew two hundert years ago what I'm jist learnin': that farmin' is a downright loosin' preposition.

Instead ev'rybody spent their time skinnin' ev'rythin' else alive. And I'm not sure yer av'rage Injian din't git some hairy idees from yer white man. Have you ever watched them scallopers out there in front of yer Make Believe Gardens in their Stanley Cups?

Yer Great Intender

King Louie, Fourteen, was yer son-king till he took over the bizness from his father, Louie the unlucky Thirteen. Young Louie he changed the Cuebec peckin' order by sendin' out a boss sibilant servant called yer Super Intender. This sure took the steam outta yer Guvner who was mostly fer show anyways, bein' nothin' more than yer King's prawn. And yer Intender was s'posed to be a kinda bufferin state 'tween the Guv and yer Bishop what was in charge of leadin' the speertuals.

Now yer Great Intender that'd be Tellon. Jean-yer-Baptist Tellon, and he figgered the best way to git people back to the land was to give them all guvermint land grabs. First off, he made some older inn-habitants into Seniors, so's yer Seniory citizens could git land by the river and pass on it over to their sons and daughters hairs. Mind you there warn't too many daughters about, so yer Tellon scouts over in France rounded up a buncha girl orfins called yer King's Daughters. Of course Louie so far had no childern of his own to speak of, not till he was Louie fifteen or sixteen. So all these unmothered marryers was brung out holesail one winter when it was so cold some batchelors was even thinkin' of gittin' married.

'Sides, there was a pole tacks on batchelors of ten pounds** a piece . . . which could run into quite a bit, dependin' how bizzy a batchelor you was.

Natcherly it bein' so cold, the fattest girls got hitched first, but it warn't long before the hole batch got got rid of, 'cause there was a lotta soldiers from the regimen of yer Carryon Salers who'd bin thinkin' of the girls behind they left. Before you knew it yer entire she-bang was dubbled up to keep warm.

** Weighty Feetnote: Yer French word fer pound is livre, and you'd be surprised at the number there was of loose livres.

Tellon he wanted to raise somethin' else in the place 'sides furs and fish. And he did too. People. That was what you'd call nowadays yer copulation explosion. If yer innerested in statistickleticks, yer habitants of Cuebec growed up from less'n five thousand to more'n five million in jist two hundert year. (Valeda says, no wonder them men and women of Cuebec think it's time to seprate.)

Jean-yer-Baptist Tellon inspectin' the sight fer yer 1676 Olymphian Games

Young Etenny Groolay, one of yer voyeurs-de-boys

Yer Voyeurs

Not ev'ry one of them French phesants wanted to git married and keep their feat parrylel to the ground while they raised a few hectors of land by the river with yer coloniac irrigation. There was a buncha pups wanted to raise more'n hectors! They wanted to whoop it up all night long in yer northern bushes and debotch things up with the Injians. I don't think they was out fer more'n a furry canew trip and a darn good time. But them Voyeurs (as they called the old-time bunny chasin' Hugh Heffers of that time) without knowin' what they was doin' had made their way acrost North 'Merka uncoverin' most of the continence.

The first of them'd be the young lad worked fer Sam Plain as Chief Boy Scout, Etenny Groolay. Young Et, he was the Great Laker of his time, bein' the first whitey to pass Ureon, Speerier, and Ontaryo altho' you can't blame him fer what happen to Eery.

He was oney a young slip of a tad when he started out, but he never got over playin' Injian. They finely got fed up with him one night hard by Lake Simcoe when he was first course on a menyou mainly made up of Cannibal's Soup.

A coupla Three Riverers name of Rattysun and Grossyears got further afeeled into the inferior. They come back to Montreal fuzzy to the gunnels with more skins than Holt Renfrew, but not havin' a huntin' license they was both fined fer bein' gamey and off-season.

Well sir, them two swamp-swingers was so mad they flipped. And they flipped right over to the Anglish side of the fence where they was welcomed as the first French seprators willin' to help skim the cream offa the top of Canada.

Yer Bay Buy

Charlie Eleven of Angland was the swinger-King that Rattysun and Grossyears swung over to. Valeda claims he was oney yer Second, 'cause his father (a chopper rather than a swinger) was Charlie One.**

Anyways, Charlie yer whatever-his-number was one of yer big givers of mink coats to such chlorines as Nell Grim who used to keep him awake with a thousand and one fairy tales. So when our two Frenchy voyeurs told the King and his proxy that the further north you go, the better the hair is on yer royl vermin, he pricked up the ears under his Dienell wig.

Upto then, Charlie and his Nellie had bin kinda board sittin' there on the throne with nothin' partickler on. The year before they'd had yer Great Fire when there was a hot time in the hole town one night, and the year before that was yer Great Pubonic Plaig, which is the old time word fer yer industerearial pollyution. But this year there was nothin' to watch but the meerahs on the sealing. So both yer Monarch and his flour was ready fer some action in furrin' parts.

Charlie got his kid brother, Prince Ruppert, a local peer with a good head, fer to work out the d-tails, and he was the one thunk up the big words on yer charter fer to give 'em all a Great Hairy Monopply on yer skin game.***

Nelly she was all fer it, but yer King was one liked to play the feeled and warn't too keen on the one shot bizness. But when they

---

** Wriggle Feetnote: Valeda claims he was only yer Second, because his Father was the Charles yer First. . . . They always put the King's numbers in yer Roamin' numerals. My gol, what'll them Eyetalians be thinkin' of next?

*** Fancy Feetnote: "Be it known, buy all these presents, oyeah, oh yeah . . ."

showed him he'd git out of it at least two prize skins from the
Beaver lodge, a coupla Elk, and mebbe a Moose or a Rotarian, he
signed up all them Gentlemen Debenturers down to yer Lowest
Common Factor. And in return fer yer match pair of beaver 'n elk,
all the Gents wanted in return was Northern Cuebec and Ontaryo,
yer Prayery Provinces, and the nice parts of yer North-West Terri-
torials.

They took acrost a nice ketch, yer Nunsotch, and it give them a
purty good Hudson Bay sail fer openers. And they soon met a few
Injians willin' to unpelt theirselves fer somethin' in exchange and
a tiny totter rum.

Well them Bay Days got so poplar, the French hadda git into
yer Likker Act too. Yer Voyeurs become delivery-de-boys and brung
it right to yer wig-warm's door fer a pelt. One of them travailin'
salesmen, yer Seer de Lavenderlaundry porridged his canew acrost
la prayery from Mitchell-a-mackinaw to Lake Winnipeg-eye-oasis.

The hole bizness made yer natives yer middlemen 'tween the
two sides, and they found it hard to choose, but it was made easier
by Mrs. Injian who liked the buys 'round the Bay and was allus
willin' to take a chance on a blanket.

Yer Frontnack

The French fella what changed the pitcher of things'd be Count yer Frontnack, yer steamed Guvner of Cuebec. But he warn't near so steamed as that High Bishop Level, who kept tryin' fer to git Frontnack to *reggie less alcools*, which means controllin' yer likker.

But yer Frontnackers won out over yer W.R.C.T.U. 'cause church is church but bizness is bizness. And next thing you know, there was a lotta fur-baring Injians that was well hung-over. Yer head-quarters of yer furryer trade was Montreal but Frontnack set up the hindquarters in Ontaryo hard by Kingston. All it was then was yer Fort Catterasstrophy; at that time yer Pen was not yet mitey as yer Sord. But with a wet bar in the Fort, yer early Ontaryo was a place to grow, even if you couldn't stand.

By this time there was a offal rivery goin' on with yer Boston States, and yer nobel Injian was caught in the middle, summers 'tween yer rum and brandy. Since rum was cheaper, yer Anglish got their furs quicker. You take yer av'rage New Anglander he went to church all the time on Sundys, but the rest of the week he warn't above edgin' on yer Eeryquoit tribes to likker-up and go on yer rampage up and down yer St. Lorrent, and sometimes git into the sackin' too. When yer Injian got rummed-up he was capable of burnin' ev'rythin' in site 'cept a second morgidge. Even downtown Montreal was fulla fire sales. And if you was a habitant livin' in yer rurals, you purty near had to sleep with yer foul piece beside you.

Frontnack never took this lyin' down. He was an old soldier of missfortune, and he retalianated by sendin' his own contra-band of Injians down to yer main part of New Angland fer to assalt and radish them clammydiggers.

But there was another way 'round them Angled-Sacksons, and that was to Go West, Old Man, which Frontnack musta heard from some in-voices jist like Jonah Vark. So he sent out his woods-

Yer French frier, Father Hennypenny at Nagger Falls

craftsmen, them bein' fellas who were purty crafty in the woods . . . what they called in French yer *curios de boys.*

One of yer more curious curios was Father Hennypenny, a French frier. He was snoopin' 'round one day hard by yer Queenson Hites when all of a sudden he heard a great roar. Well, yer Hennypenny thought the sky was fallin' before he went 'round the bend and seen yer Nagger Falls. He liked the spot so much, he hung around and started divertin' yer local Injians into bein' Christyans. If he'd gotten them into yer state of holy acrimony he'd bin able to start yer Nagger Falls tooriest bizness all that sooner.

Frontnack even sent his gal, La Sal, on the road. When she hit the banks of yer Missysippy she finely got down in the mouth, hung 'round waitin' fer some action, and one night got shot in yer Latin Quarters.

It was that swish-buckler, yer Seer Deeperbill stirred things up the most. He musta bin yer Errall Flinn of his day dashin' all over the lots, sneakin' a comandoe raid on yer Hudson Bay post facters, and even makin' it hot fer them Florider Spanish down Pepsacola way. He too trucked over to Norleens fer some snugglin' and finely claimed Lucy Anna fer yer King of France, altho' whether he ever got a piece of it fer his trouble is one of histry's mistrys.

But by the time Frontnack got thru sendin' out his travailin' salesmen, yer French lilies was blowin' all the way out Thunder Bay way and down to yer Mecksican Golf.

That was when the Anglish woke up to the fack that they was bein' slowly but surely encirclesized. Mind you, yer French thought the Anglish was doin' the same thing to them. So fer a time both sides skulked 'round the other like two picky-pockets in a revolver door.

51

Yer Repulsion of Yer Excadians

All tolled, there was oney a hundert thousand of yer Frenchies all over, so by goin' down on yer Missysippy they was spreadin' theirselves offal thin even if they got laid end to end.

Whereas yer New Anglishers was more'n a million and a haff people per square head, and all of 'em stuffed into thirteen unlucky colonists. So somethin's gotta give, as they say at the Department of Wealth and Hellfare.

Land was gittin' to be even more poplar than fur by this time. Mebbe it was that reel estate boom started off by the famous French dancer Tally Rand and his Southsea Bubbles. Anyways, yer thirteen Anglish columnists wanted to git in on it too, so they started yer War of yer Spanish Sucksession. I dunno what any of yer Spanish had to do with it, but yer Anglishmen sure knew his onions when it come to makin' war. When that excuse give out, they started yer War of yer Osterian Sucksession, and don't ask me how them Osterizers got drug into it.

Anyways, yer upshat of the hole thing was that the Birtish got back Newfieland and Novy Scotia which was at that time called Excadia.** Now most of the people livin' 'round those parts at that time was French-speakin', and it's kinda frustratin' fer to conker and then find out there's a lotta forners still livin' there. There was oney one thing to do ... kick 'em out without so much as a buy-yer-leave.

So yer Halluvagonians come in and asked all them Ex-cadience to swear at them with an Oaf of Yer Legions. Now you take yer av'rage Cape Bertoner he's pretty strick Nitesa Clumbuss and din't

** Short-formed Feetnote: Mainly on accounta they was soon to become ex-Canadians.

wanta change dance halls in mid-stream. All in all, the hole thing was a pretty teery-jerky show.

If youse wanta read the story 'bout it, Henry Wordsworth has writ a long fellow of a pome about what went on in yer Minus Basin with one of yer Grand Prey girls called Evaseline. Her boyfriend slipped away from her, and then she was put up fer export too, and neither one of 'em met up till they was both on sociable securities and not able to do much about rekindlin' their sparks.

The main thing to remember 'bout all this was, it was yer Anglish and not yer French what started this Seprator bizness.

Yer Wolf at Yer Back Door

Not all of yer ex-Cadience was took over by yer Anglish. Up in Cape Berton hard by yer Brass Door Locks was this big Fortress called Louieburg. Now don't ask me why a lady fort had a fella's name, but all them Louieburgers was holed up-tite in there and the Birtish couldn't even get at them with their navel blockhead.

'Sides that, yer French had a General, Mucky de Mountclam, who was a snorter of a millytant. And altho' he was outnumbed mebbe umpteen to one, he kept beatin' the Birtish all over. He beat off three Birtish prongs who attacked him hard by Nagger Falls, Tiecountyeryoga, and Ossawaywego, till there was an uproar in yer London Common House.

Yer Premeer, Will Pit, kept gittin' the blame fer all this from yer Birtish M.P.P.'s. It warn't dreckly his falt, but I guess they all needed a Pit to hiss at. What yer Birtish generals was short on was branes, so Pit permoted a young whippin'-snapper with no chin but a nose could hoe turnips. Well sir, this young pup (he was part Wolf on his father's side) was give the job of beseechin' Cuebec till they give in.

But yer Guvner of Cuebec was yer Marquest de Vaudeville and he figgered he was impregnant. He evaccinated ev'rybody from the Lower Town and had them all on their Uppers in no time. He brung back yer General Mountclam from the Marrytime farm team, and figgered all they hadda do was hole up in yer Shadow Frontnack till freeze-up, which in Cuebec comes shortly after Laboured Day.

Now below them in yer river was Wolf, and he knew he hadda reach fer the top soon after the kids was back in scool, when Hull freezes over. He rented a boat and went up and down yer river after dark with muffled ores.**

** Wrapt Feetnote: In those days yer nitrates was cheaper.

Genral Wolf lookin' acrost to yer Planes of Abie-ham hard by yer Shadow Frontnack

Wolf was a great reader in scool and had heard 'bout yer Greeks and yer Trudgin' Horse. He ast himself what yer Greeks woulda done this time, and that's where he got the idee of goin' in the back way.

Jist upriver from yer Shadow Frontnack-on-the-Rocks was this big crack called yer Wolf's Cave. Wolf he figgered it was a lucky sign to find a crack with his name on it, and he din't care weather there was a real wolfe in that cave or no. He figgered him and his soldyers could heist theirselves up into yer Planes of Abieham.

Jist before they went up yer crack, Wolf resited a piece of memmory work from back in scool:

> Rosaries red, violence blue
> Mornin' glories on yer grave
> I love you.**

Wolf said at the time he'd druther of writ that pome than take on Cuebec, but somebody nudged him from behind with a baynet, and up he went.

As soon as him and them Grenadine Gards clum to the top, they run acrost a few pickets on duty and powered-over 'em. You take yer av'rage picket, yer bound to run into a few, 'cause somebody in Cuebec is allus on strike.

There was a ring-dang-slam-bang battle fer a quarter of an hour when Mountclam led his small farce agin yer Wolfmen, but before the end of the first period both captins was morally wounded. Game was called on accounta dark, Mountclam was carried off the field by yer Nurselin Sisters and become amortized, and yer Tedium was sung by the quire.

Mountclam lost yer battle as well, but them Nurselin nones thought him such a good head they keep it in a glass case even today. As fer yer Wolf, he was give a big send-off post-humorously by Roylty, but I'll bet he'd ruther of had yer roylty from that pome he recit.

** Dogrel Feetnote: Writ, Valeda b'leeves, by Edgar Guess.

57

Yer After-Mass

The thing what really defeeted Cuebec was the fack that nobody in France give a darn about it. Ev'ry hatterer in Paris was up to hair in beavers and what else was Canada good fer? Yer French King Louie the Next, he was more innerested in yer Lesser Aunt Tillies and the West Undies.

When yer Paris Piece Treat was co-sined by all sides, all King Louie wanted to keep of us was yer two Newfie aisles of Sam Peeair and Mickey Long. I guess he jist wanted a place where he'd git cognack and cheap purefumes and that stuff that makes yer heart grow fonder — yer absinth.

So it was yer Old French what left out in the lurch yer New French. All them high mucky-mucks in charge got out of Cuebec and took French leave back home: yer Guvner Vaudeville, yer Intended Bigot, and even yer Seer de Levis packed his jeans and ran. That left behind jist yer habitants, yer R.C. church people, and a few seniors.

And who d'you think took charge of the drivin' seat? 'Twarn't yer Birtish conkers, fer none of them could speak yer by-lingo. It was yer Jesyouwait priests acted up as yer inter-middlary and before they got thru, you could go to a Bingo in downtown Mont-real any nite of the week.

I guess yer Anglish figgered they wanted the bizness end of yer Cuebec and they din't care too much what yer frog does on Sunday. (That's what they started to call themselves about this time. I never could figger it out but Valeda says it's 'cause they wore coats with long tails. I thought that'd make them pollywogs, but Valeda says no, in the old time days they all wore frog coats and cutaway pants. Then I asked her if we was called Wasps on accounta yer long stingers, and she told me to shut up and write histry.)

58

Yer 'Merken Risin' Up

Well, no sooner had they got yer Frenchies rapped than some outlyin' Injians started shakin' their tailfeathers. You take yer Illnoise and Ohiyuh tribe, they was never too parshul to yer Anglishman anyways. Probly 'cause the French treated them better . . . or more offen.

Anyways, the Injians was lookin' fer a good cheerleader so soon's they got this new Pontiac they headed strait for Deetroit and whooped up a lacrotch match with yer locals. Now this here was a game to make yer hair stand on end. Yer first half ended in some close shaves since yer Injians was usin' tommy-hocks 'stead of lacrostics.

As far as yer Birtish went it was a garrison finish: Cleveland Injians 0, Deetroit Lyons 22. Yer Birtish Umpire called the game on accounta mayhemp, and the next season yer Redskins was drummed outta the leeg fer ruffin'. Pontiac, he was arrested on general motives and had to give a total recall.

I guess the fun never sets on yer Birtish Umpire. No sooner was the "red mennis" put down than up sprung all that Yanky hanky panky. Yer King of Angland that time was George yer Hundert and 'Leventh.** I'm not sure what started the ruckus this time, but them Yanks had never got on too well with the Mother's country ever since they was Prodigal Fathers and had to come acrost.*** Now they all come over here so's they could warship as they seen fit, and tried to git ev'rybody else to purify God in the same way.

** Dienasty Feetnote: Now that don't make no sense to me neither but Valeda says it's a case of Roamin' Noomerals agin. Wish they'd sit still.

*** Bunion's Feetnote: All this is more ackuratly recoded in Yer Pill-grim's Progress.

Well, by the time George yer three I's got his turn on the thrown, nobody was payin' much attention to him, and sendin' parsels thru yer post without stamps. The King he got mad and invited them all to his Royl Party at the Boston Gardens and put tacks in their tea. But Valeda says yer Yanks is all alkyholics-unanimus, so in the middle of the party they all got overbored and threw up the tea into the harbour.

When George heard about this he was fit to be tied, and the vicey of yer versey too, him bein' madder'n a haddock and spendin' quite a bit of his time at the foolish farm. He got so mad he put his foot down on them Yanks with yer Stamp Tacks, so that by the end of yer fisical year 1776 nobody was even aloud a nickel on the Declaration of yer Dependants.

Well, most of yer Yanks succeeded. They sent George a telly-gram what said: "Up *yer* Union, Jack!" and got their own flag made by a little old woman, Bitsey Ross.**

Soon's they could, them Congersmen drew up yer Billy Rites, sayin' what they wanted was an open convent freely arrived at. Things got worser in Boston when some demon straters was hurt at Lexinton and Conkerd, which musta bin one offal bizzy innersection.

One of yer Massychewsets Ruffriders, Pall Reveer, got off his high horse to warn all in the family yer Birtish was comin' fer dinner when the north light hit the old Archy-beakon on Bunker's Hill.

Pall Reveer had three horse lost under him, one by land and two by seize, and a forth went thru his clothes. It hit an inner-cent stand-by, Nate Inhale, who became dead which proved

---

** Far and Wide Feetnote: Later adopted by Congersmen at yer Conti-nental Congers (altho' most of yer members come oney from one of the five).

fatal. He is still dead and still famous for sayin' under his last breadth: "I'm glad I have oney one life to give fer my country."

Valeda don't b'leeve we should dwell with George Warshinton leavin' Mount Vermin to forge fer himself in the valley and sleep around the hole country till he become yer father of it. She says the oney thing as is worth notin' is that the Yank rebellyun tried to git us in Canada to join in their frackass. The funny thing of all is that it was yer Anglishmen in Montreal was the ones willin' to seprate down to yer States. But yer av'rage French-Canadian, him as is s'posed to be loyl oney to yer Pope, was the one staid loyl to yer Anglish King! How about that fer yer thought fer the day? I guess it takes all kinds to keep a country together, and that time we was held by yer French connection.

Our Yankys Come Home

Now the Birtish General in all this too-do was yer Lord Corn-haulus — him as lost the toss when Warshinton threw the silver dollar acrost yer Potomack River.** The Birtish squares extinguished themselves on yer feeled of battle when they formed up their pantaloons and fell, never to rise agin.

After the Birtish got demobbed by yer rebels and went back home, there was still a buncha Yanks down in yer States that wasn't too pro-Yanky. They was still singin' "God Save Yer King" while the rest-of 'em was standin' up fer "My Country, What's It To Thee?"

Now these pro-Birtish Yanks was called Torees. Don't ask me what they had to do with them Retrogressive Preservatives havin' their national party nowadays, 'cept that yer old-time Toree he too was allus kickin' agin the guvermint and never seem to git out of yer Loyl Opposite Position.

But the main kick yer pro-Yanky Yanks had agin yer Toree was they never did bare arms on yer 'Merken side. That made them in the eyes of Oncle Sam, nothin' better'n drafty dodges. And they was put thru the mill fer it, lemme tell you. Even if some of 'em was realy unconscious objectors, that din't make no never mind to yer paterotic Stars and Strippers. Matter of fack, quite a few Torees 'fore they got over yer Marrytime boarders was tar and fettered.

After yer War when yer Congersmen in Phillydelphi brung out yer Billy Rites after their Constitootional, they never said nothin' in it 'bout no am-nasty fer yer drafty vaders. So hardly none of them Torees wanted to come back States-side.

So that's how we come to git our first batcha Yanks. And

** Tricky Feetnote: Valeda tells me yer dollar went a lot further in them days.

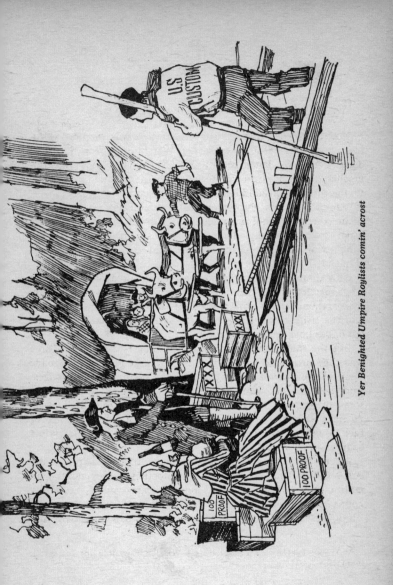

Yer Benighted Umpire Roylists comin' acrost

they staid too. Their was so many of 'em, they started a hole province of their own, New Brunsick. Up to that time it was jist a buncha fiddleheads growin' wild.

Even today them old-time Yanks git together and have a meetin' of yer Benighted Umpire Roylists once in a while — a buncha true bloors who still think King George the Hundert and 'Leventh is the cat's peejamas. It's easy to tell yer av'rage Roylist when he's in yer men's washroom at the end of a moovy. He's the one stands up fer yer National Antrum even when his pants is at haff mast.

Yer Upper and Yer Lower, Yer Bertha Two Nations

Some of them Umpire Roylists went even further than be-comin' New Brunsickers. They spread theirselves all over yer Atlantic sideboard. Some crost over to yer Cape Berton and inter-bread with yer High Scotch. Others din't wanta go that far but stopped short in Novy Scotia and become Antigoni-sticks.**

A buncha yer Roylists went the other way and squattied down hard by Shurebrook in yer Far East Townships. And that's where we run into yer yuman racism.

Now there's often-times yer French and yer Anglish can't stand each other on accounta they never herd sich langridge. But also with yer Roylist, most of 'em was of yer Anglecan religion and din't wanta go near yer R.C. church which b'leeved in sich things as yer Lost Rites with Extreme Moncton.

To make things worse, over in France they jist had a Revela-tion of their own and a lotta aristocats was comin' out to Cuebec to make more Frenchmen.

Yer French Revelation was started by yer "Sans Cool-hots" — a buncha commoner Paris people with no pants on.*** They riz up agin their nobel overlorders and kicked them outta their chapeaus. Then they marched on yer palisades and declared the hole King Family null and void. They even decomposed yer King and Queen itself. King Louie in sweet Sixteen and Marie Handtonette in the next apartment was rounded up by leaps and bound, put in tumblers and then gelatined.

** Sack-religion Feetnote: Valeda says she never cared fer yer Anti-gonistick, fer they're the ones aren't too sure they b'leeve in God.

*** Radickle Feetnote: Valeda thinks they was revoltin'!

66

Now all this was done in the name of "Liberty, Fertility, Maternity." That's why a lotta exiles and priests come out to Cuebec to find a new life fer theirselves, their childern, and their antsesters. And bein' French, they soon learned to make both ends meat.

Natcherly, this made Cuebec more French than ever, so a lotta yer Benighted Roylists wanted to pick up their belongin's and shuffle back to Buffalo. But most of 'em jist moved to the sublurbs west of yer Mount Royl where they become to be called West Mounters. But some moved even further west in Cuebec, all the way from yer Bay of Quinzy down to Sarnya-Winser way.**

About this time we also got a big batcha Scotch, Persbyteerians who didn't mind yer French churchgoer havin' a place to neel as long as they had a seprate place to stand. That's how the place got divided into two kind of Canadians — yer Upper and yer Lower. It din't mean one was better'n the other 'cause it warn't a case of yer shanty French and yer lace curtin Anglish. In them days nobody had lace curtins and ev'rybody had to use the shanty.

** Ticklish Feetnote: It's hard fer Valeda to b'leeve that at one time we was all inside yer Cuebec boarders, 'cause that's what us Ontary-aryans has allus bin afraid of.

Yer Scotch Come Acrost

It was about this time our country got loaded with Scotch. They flocked over here in drovers 'cause back home in their lairds someone found out you could make more money raisin' sheep than Scotchmen, on accounta you can skin a sheep more'n once.

The first batch was penned up in the hole of a ship and brung over by one of yer overlards, yer Erl of Sellchurch. He took them over, spread them in klans all acrost our land, till they took us over.**

Yer Hyland klansmen was lookin' fer a nice flat place to curl up fer the winter and swing their stones. So they settled down beside yer Lake Winnipeg-eye-oasis, spread their seed, and started yer Red River serial.

It was yer Hudson Bay street sharpers sold them this land, never tellin' them there was already a hole clumpa Crees on it. This led to quite a micks-up. Sometimes yer Scotty got along with yer Cree and sometimes not. When they finely did git friendly, what come outen the hole thing was what they call bein' "Matey." We'll git to later when they got along worse, 'cause yer riel trubble is yet to come.

Most of yer Scotch was settlers, but there was one or two had the wanderin' foot trubble and went further west to git in on yer Rocky fur trade. One of 'em, Alex Sandy McKinsey, was the first to paddle hisself all the way acrost yer trans-Canada. When he run outta river he'd jist pick up his punt and porridge the prayery.

** Kiltick Feetnote: Valeda says yer Scotch was took in, not took over. She is low Scotch up to the kilt. She was Valeda Drain that was, one of the old Flesherton Drains, but she was a Drain on her father's side, and gits her Scotch from her mother.

Alex Sandy McKinsey, uncoverin' yer Specific Ocean

He got fooled once into goin' too far north by yer Boring Alice hard by Aurora. He was mebbe thinkin' they was lights from yer Caligary Stampeed. But he made a fresh chart and with the help of Percy Veerence got all the ways out to Vancoover 1793 B.C.**

Took him best part of six months and by that time his hair was offal long. Valeda says that's why he come back right away, she don't b'leeve yer Vancoover mare let him stay. There's a pitcher of him givin' yer V fer Victry sign, and yer mare oney givin' him the haff of it back.

The main thing, it was yer Scotchman found yer cheap charter root acrost Canada from Mare to Mare.***

** Recurd Feetnote: Agin, Before Confederation.

*** Bury-crattick Feetnote: Valeda phoned them up in the Infocan. to find out what yer "A Mare Usque Ad Mare" meant on yer Canadian Shield, and they told her it was "From Yer C.B.C.," but my gol, them fellas wasn't radio-active in them days.

Yer Evasion from Yer Eweass

Now that they was two sepratist countries, Canada and yer U.S. of A. started puttin' up boarders and makin' sure each other hadda go thru some strange customs.

But there was some Yanks thought Canada by rites belonged to them. They was a buncha Warshinton Capitolists called yer "War Hocks." They b'leeved in somethin' called yer "Many-fist Dustiny" which meant that if us Canuckers din't wanta become another star in their flag, they'd roll up their fistick cuffs, dust off their nuckles, and give us a few stripes of our own.

And they meant it. I fergit how the hole offal thing started. Some Yanky gum-boat had a shot-put acrost yer stern of one of our frigits. At the time the rest of yer Royl Navy was all tied up on yer playin' fields of Eaton's agin yer new French upstarter, Napolio Bonuspart. Yer Birtish Jack-in-the-Tar finely beat yer French navvies at Trafalgar Square where they all went down to the Waterloo.

But that was no help to us, left with three thousand mile of fenceless boarder. Mind you, yer Yank high-ups warn't too smart in their stragedy. It woulda bin easy to git sneakers acrost all parts of yer boarder, but yer U.S. general marched bold as his brass acrost yer Piece Bridge and rite up to yer nearest Laura Seacord.

Now Laura she warn't content to sit around like one of yer fanny farmers. As soon as them Yanks set down to eat her outta house and store, she snuck out to the cow barn and decided to pull somethin'. She took out her prize cow, yer local Dairy Queen, and rode it more'n twenty mile barebones. When she got

Laura Seacord passin' around her goodies at the camp of her General, 1. Sick Brock

to her General, I. Sick Brock, she told him the Yanks was comin', "over there."**

Well sir, Brock he jist waited in yer am-bushes till them Yanks got to the Hite of yer Queenson hard by yer Hydro. Then he let them have it right in the rear-gard and beat the retreat offa them. Sad to say he got hisself nicked in the frackass when a bullit bounced offa Rick O'Shay and give our General the rigger's morse.

But a greatful country soon remembers, and the both of 'em, yer Brave Brock and yer fine upstandin' Holsteen farm woman, got to be immoral. And they're both still in bizness today, fer she's a box of choclits and he's a hotel.

There's some Yanks as won't admit it, but when you score up all the fights in that war, it finely come out fer us Canadians, 18-12. But that should give yer U.S. some satisfactional, on accounta now they don't have to say that the first time they ever lost a war was in South Viet Napam.

** Tired Feetnote: "Over there" was yer Beaver's Damn now called yer town of Thorhold, but still known by many a visiter as that dam backwater.

Yer Fur Murge

After we got them Yanks settled in their hash, our Scotchmen started givin' us trubble. Them fuzzy-need curlers all seemed to clan up together, but that don't mean they git along with their-selves. There's two differnt Scotches, yer Highs and yer Lows, and they like nothin' better than usin' each other as sporrin' partners. Once in a while they'd lay into one another till some-body got kilt. You take yer av'rage Hairy Louder type Scotchman, I think they's worse'n yer Irish fer hallin' off and rapin' one another over the coles.**

Out West at that time most of yer Scotch was up to their dirks in fur. They took over yer Montreal fur trait after them French got becalmed by our General Wolf. After yer 18-12 War, no traiters could go down to the States any more lookin' fer pelt. Yer Yank fur don't wear too long anyways, mebbe 'cause the animals had already wore it fer a long time first. But also, the colder she is outside the thicker yer fur, so them clanny Scotch traiters headed north and west. This was right up yer Hudson Baystreeter's alley, and both companies soon found out "two's a crowd."

But that never stopped yer Northwest Scotch, fer when it come to makin' money them fellas'd cut yer throat behind yer back. Valeda don't b'leeve me but that's what they done to Lord Sellchurch's Red Riverers, and they was their own flesh and bones — all Scotch and a yard wide. You'll mind I said before, Lord Sellchurch had bought land fer his Hyland handy-crofters

---

** Cross Feetnote: Valeda's mad at me. She thinks that word should be *rake*. But when them Scotch git their dandruff up, it's never no common operation. Mind you, rape's not what she used to be. Nowadays it's some-thin' yer Ottawa planners want us farmers to git into so's we won't waste our time growin' wheat.

at the coroner of yer Winnypeg and yer Assinnerboys; they soon found out there was already a buncha haff-broods livin' there in rude huts.**

Some of them haff-broods was haff-Scotched. You take yer av'rage Winnypeg winter, it was purty much the same as now, and the oney way to keep yer wig warm was to dubble up intense. That's how a lotta Injian women with feathers up their hair and pigtails down their backs was called "Mac" or "Mc". In fack there's still a hole tribe of Scotch Injians called yer McMacs.

But them Matey haffbroods din't know what to make of this new bunch comin' in to their Red River nomad's land all tartaned-up in their Tammy Chanters. First thing these new Canadians done was to put up fences and told the buffalo to shuffle off. Now yer Matey he was never one fer fencin' around; he was purty near allus a gypsee and nowadays he'd probly git arrested fer fragrancy. And as fer yer buffalo, that was his stable food. All them haff-broods needed fer their three squares a day was a coupla pemmy-cans (sorta cold buffalo burgers with razzberry juice fer ketchup).

You seen this happen before in yer av'rage Holyrood moovy. There's allus two kinds, yer settlers and yer unsettlers — yer wild cattle rusters and yer sheepish bunch. The fack that this time there was some Scotch on both sides din't seem to matter a damsite. Why even today down in Novy Scotia them Cape Berton Hylanders git lickered up and start tossin' their tellyfone polls at each other.

But things got so bad 'tween yer Mannytober fur-Scotch and yer farm-Scotch, they even had a mass-acker. It was hard by a place called Seven-Ups where one day yer uncooler heads pre-

---

** Upright Feetnote: Valeda says them haff-broods was good Cathlicks and musta had some nice sayin's on their walls as well, plus pitchers of saints with their hearts showin' on the outside.

77

veiled. Yer settlers was drawin' lots fer lots when all of a sudden out come yer Mateys rollin' their war-hoops and shoutin' "Scots Wahoo!" Din't take long, but a lotta Scots shot lotsa shots at a lotta other Scots, and the oney one to come outta this free-assco ahead of the game was the fella cuts the epigrams on yer toomstones.

Yer settler's boss, Erl of Sellchurch, was at the time up to sue Saint Marie. He was tryin' to hire some Swish mercy-marys fer to come back and fill them Norwestern haff-broods fulla holes. But he was too late. Yer massage was over and yer dam-nage was done. Sellchurch he tried to sue fer liable both yer Hudson Bayers and yer Norwest Furco, but before it got to legitation he took sick with the TB (or not TB, that's still the question), become fatal ill and woke up one mornin' dead.

Mind you, same thing happen to yer Norwesters the next year. Their Furco went outta bizness when their bank rupted and they went into the hands of yer deceevers. They was took over by Hudson Bay, whose boss at that time was Sir George Simp & Son.** After the two companies become one joint, ev'rybody become buddy-buddy, like yer Three Mousekyteers — it was one fur all and all fur one.

** Left Feetnote: Simp's sons was born outta headlock. When he hired help his slogan was "Yule enjoy eaton with Simp's sons."

Rufflin' It In Yer Bush

Well sir, first it was fish and fur, then it was wood and whisky brung in the money. Some of yer first famblys of Uppity Canada was our booze makers too, them same mucky-mucks as is now high up in the foreflush of yer cafeteeria sassiety.

Seems like mosta the trees was chopped down to make barrels for yer stave trade. Then they got filled up with home-brew rot-gut, and it was drunk by the same lumberin' jacks chopped down the trees. To git more money fer a bender they hadda go back and cut down more trees, makin' it a kinda viscous sickle of perpetulant emotion.

It was yer Irish was yer biggest lumberers. They was driven out of yer Potato Farmin' in Ireland after yer spuds give out. That was when them absentee-minded landlards from Angland started plantin' Irishmen instead.

So yer Irish steeraged their way over to yer Ottawa Valley and tried to settle down. But the place was already fulla the same kinda starchy Anglishmen had et all their potatos back home. From then on there was never any settlin' yer Irish. Ev'ry Saturday night in Arnprior or Carp, it was a ring-tailed snorter of a Highburnyin not-so-fancy-dress brawl.

Yer Anglish squire-leaders stuck up their noses at sich sheeny-annigans. They was all purty much like that fambly on the TV had all the hot flashbacks, yer Whitefolks of Jellna. One of 'em, a right moody woman, writ a book about how hard it was to be a pieinear lady in them days and wear ruffles in yer bush. Her husband was one of yer Officer's Messes — tryin' to be one of them gentleman farmers can't raise nothin' but their hats. All they ever did was complaint, them two; life with them musta bin one long quittin' bee. But *she* griped over farmers what done well, callin' them yer Commoner Man without no edification.**

It was about this time Great-Grandpa Farquharson shipped out here with yer Orange drove from North Ireland. He din't wanta micks with yer left-foot Dogan Irish, so he tried out yer homestead life hard by Lake Simpco. This was a buncha cottiges run by grave John Simpco, I b'leeve the same one run that depart mental store down in Tronto.***

They was nice people yer Simpcos, but offal name droppers. They even called two hole townships after their dogs, Tiny and Tay. Valeda's glad they never got no further north or we'd be now likely livin' in Rover or Spot Township.

Now Great-Gramma din't like stayin' 'round those parts 'cause she was a Westly Methadist and the oney church there was fer yer Anglecans who was so High they spent mosta their time on their nees. The Farquharsons left when they was told that the oney ministers for Method people 'round them parts was yer odd Circus Rider.

Great Grampa and Gramma moved up Georgian Bay way jist this side of Pointa Barrel. Here they started stumpin' and log-rollin' and even makin' their own soap. Many's the night they staid up till sunrise smokin' pot-ash. Later they moved to a log house with wall-to-wall floors, which ain't standin' no more but would be now right inside yer Metra-popolitan Parry Sound on the Fourth Concession down by the Town Line not far from the old Orr House.

** Long Feetnote: Well my gol, what good has all that Edgy Ryerson book stuff done anyways? What's the use of studyin' up on Animal Husbandry when you know yer stock is goin' to make their own arrangements? Or why try that artifishy insinuation when the cattle prefer draft to the bottled stuff? I tell you the oney good thing I got from scool was learnin' to sign my own name, otherwise I'd have to pay cash.

*** Editor's Feetnote: Honest? (Ed.)

Grave John Simpco overseein' the bildin' of the new York City Hall

Yer Fambly Compack and Yer Littlest Rebel

Now this here's not about cars; it's about somethin' else that should be recalled reg'lar. The hole trubble with farmers today started more 'n a hundert years ago when yer city people started pushin' us around. And they're still doin' it even now, what with all them big capitolist tyfoons like Bob Loblaw or yer A & P Taylor buyin' up good farm land fer to play their own brand of Monopply. By growin' their own prod-use they're forcin' us small fellas outen the holesail bizness jist like they done to yer corner stores.

That's what happen to yer Roamin' Umpire. If you don't b'leeve me look up a book called *Yer Deecline and Fallout* by that old gibbon (yer old-time historian and not yer monkey with a red and blue bottom). He claims it was yer city people squeezin' yer farmer offa his land and forcin' him to become one of yer poppers on well-fare that brung about the end of yer Westend Civilly-eye-zation all them centurions ago.

Well sir, in our own Province, there was a buncha high mucky-mucks tried that back in '37. (That'd be yer 18, not yer 19.)** In them days, yer 1837's, yer local Kosher Nostril what run Uppity Canada was called yer Fambly Compack. It was headed by Bishop Scrawn, which is spelt SCRACHIN', but you can bet he never hadda do any of that fer a livin', bein' top piller and bolster of yer High Anglecan Church. His aida-camp was John Beverly Robinson, which I dunno too much about, 'cept he sounds like he never could make up his mind whether he was a boy or girl. Last and probly least was Sir Francis Blond Head, who soon proved he had nothin' inside it.

** Back Feetnote: Yer 1937 was back when Mitch Hepburn showed how he knew his onions, and he pulled a few other things too.

These three town snobs dummynated yer guvermint and grabbed most of yer land fer theirselves what was s'posed to be used fer farmin'. These absenteasers wanted to hold on to their Crown Royl Preserves till after us farmin' fools had bilt the place up, then they'd re-zone it to yer city folks at inflammation prices jist as soon as they'd lowered yer real estate boom.

The one sty in the ointment that kept buggin' yer Family Compack was a little Low Scot name of Willy "The Lion" Mackenzie. When he roared he bugged them city snobs more 'n I do my potatos, and he done it mostly by hisself, so you have to give the little bugger credit.**

Willie run what they call yer underground newspaper, and b'leeve me that's where yer right-wing-collared Compack people wished Willy was. They hired some ruff-necks to sneak in one night and throw his tripewriter into Tronto Harbour. Well sir, Willie warn't too ankshus to git out an under-water newspaper, so he run from his office and ended up first mare of Yorkville, which even then was considered pretty far-out from the rest of Tronto.

But yer Compackers kicked him outen that job too, mainly on accounta Willy din't like their high-rise attitudes and what was gonna develop. They got him band from comin' back into town, and he hadda stay with yer sub-urbins north of yer Metra-popoli-tan limits. He spent his time gittin' drunk in Monty Gummery's Tavern, and one day when he was feelin' no pain he thunk up yer Uppity Canada Rebellyun.

A buncha other topers strung along with him, and he mustard all them stragglers down Young Street. They was all three sheets in the wind, havin' made sev'ral stops on the way, and by the time they got hard by yer Gardens, they was in no condition fer a

** Uprazed Feetnote: Valeda wasn't too sure I should call him that, but I told her that was his professional, bein' as how he was doin' it ev'ry day as a newspaper communist.

84

Willy "The Lion" MacKenzie after leavin' Monty Gummery's and headin' strait down town

face-off. That was the end of their straggle, fer they was all badly out-numbed and well hung-over. Nobody got hurt or killed tho', 'cause no one fired until they could see the whites of their eyes which by that time Willy and his fellas din't have any.

You'd think all them High Anglecan Christyans woulda fore-gave Willy and his revels like they tell you in church. But most of 'em was driv down to the States and never come back, till you'd think that Fambly Compack was the same bunch in charge of yer C.B.C.

As fer Willy the Lion, he tried evadin' Canada from the States, but the Yanks put him in jail fer disturbin' yer Piece Bridge, so Willy finely come back to Yorkville and joined yer Established Mint as jist another Member of yer House of Assendbilly.

Up Yer Pappynose!

That was quite a year yer '37 back in yer eighteens. Fer one thing it was the first time old Queen Victorya got put on her throne. It was too bad she hadda have rebiliousness in both her Uppers and her Lowers of Canada.

Yer Lowers had much the same kick as yer Uppers, namely they was gittin' the city fellas boot up their rurals too. It warn't a matter of yer Frenchy versy yer Anglish ... there was plenty of them on both sides. In fack yer French and yer Anglish farmer has pretty near allus been of the same mind when it come to gittin' the wrong end of yer manoor fork.

The funny thing was yer Church which warn't too keen on their phesants gittin' up on their hind legs and demandin' their rites. You'da thought them country people would git some support from their paris priests after goin' to church reglar ev'ry week and payin' their tiths off.**

Funnier still was that it was a city lawyer name of Louie Joe Pappynose (I guess his looks took after his father) what started yer rural balls rollin'. Lou he was already in yer Cuebec guvermint but agin yer Guvermint, sort of a not too loyl Opposite Position. He got all yer French farmers rot up till they bared their arms and sung yer "Mayonnaise."

That done it. If it's one song yer Cuebecker-in-charge was scared of, it was this one that decapassitated yer King and Queen of France. So yer Guvner suspended Abie's corpus and put Marshal Law in charge of the hole she-bang.

After that, ev'rybody was purty repressed. A lotta yer lefty hot-heads was shipped off to Austria fer to live with yer Kangy-

---

** Fisical Feetnote: Valeda don't like me sayin' that, but that's yer French word fer when they pay ten percent to give Our Lady Perpetyal help.

roos and Cola bares. (Valeda thinks mebbe it was Australalia where they go down under and wear bathin' soots all winter.) But no matter which, it was still pretty tuff on yer French-speakers when even hardly no Anglishmen can understand them Bushymen down there up under.

That's somethin' I got a thing to say about, all this by-linga-malism. A lotta people 'round our way is agin it. They don't wanta bother to "polly voo yer mamsell from armentears" when they go down to Montreal fer a good feeda garlick. When I went down fer yer Exposé in '67, I took along our boy Orville, and he helped me look up the words, and we ordered our meal in French. I said to yer waiter: "Garkon icky . . . jimmy sweeze apple Charlay Far-kew-harson ay jay desire della vee-and rose-bif aveck due pain ay la ketchup." And do you know what? That waiter he talked to the both of us in purty good Anglish fer the rest of the hole time!

So I say try. Here's what yer by-lingamalism will do fer Canada. If all us Angled-Sacksons start speakin' French it won't be no time at all before ev'ry inhabitant will come back spoutin' Anglish.

Yer Loco Motive

After we had them twin rebellyuns, in steereo so to speak, good Queen Victoryus sent out to find what was the matter with us, Lord Durm, one of her best peers.**

Durm, his job was to make a loud report on what to do with our Upper and Lower. Yer Number One Durm recommend was to join up yer French and Anglish into one province and make 'em both responsible fer guvmint. This sure din't tickle yer Frenchie to shout "Who-pee!" since the responsible part meant sharin' each other's detts, and there was already a wopper on yer Uppers.

Number Two also caused quite a bit of it to fly. It was a recommend fer a Rebellyun Lost Bill, fer to constempate them who had lost yer rebellyun and undergone suffrage durin' yer riot acts. This time it was yer Anglish kicked over the traces. Yer West Mounters marched downtown, called yer Guvner Alaclair Fontaine a rotten aig, and started arson 'round yer Place D'Ames. They even started makin' many-fistos and talked about sepratin' down to yer States.

But soon as French customers started spendin' their guvmint handouts in yer downtown stores, them Anglish merchants got down to bizness and took off their U.S. take-over bibs. Nothin' like a little cream off the top to slow down yer seprator.

Speakin' of fresh capital, Ottawa was chose as the new site fer yer nation's capitalists. Ev'rybody thought it was gonna be Tronto, known in them days as Hogtown. But Ottawa has done

---

** Private Feetnote: Valeda says I din't have to say that and how would I know sich inamit things anyways?

purty good since in that department fer a little lumberin' place oney noted fer log-rollin' and pork barellin'.**

Course it warn't called Ottawa up till then. It was bilt by a Newfie named Kernel By, and has been called By-pass. The new name, Ottawa, musta bin an old Injian word meanin' "form-committee-to-study-yer-matter."

About this time, two things come around the bend that raised a lotta steam. One was yer railroad train, invented by James What — an old Anglish kettle-man. The other was Sir Johnny Macdonald, an imported Scotch with quite a bite. Them two got together and conceeved berth fer this country.

It's hard to say whether yer coast-to-coast Canada come about 'cause of yer sea-by-sea railroad or the vicey of yer versey. It's a sorta chick-in-yer-aig argument to guess who got laid first.

Mind you, there warn't much layin' goin' on in Canada before this time. Yer States already had five thousand mile of track when us had oney fifteen-and-a-haff. But our stock started to roll when Johnny Mac got his first M.P. By the time he got into yer Cabinet (and he was allus in there) they had a railroad named after him, yer Grand Drunk.

It went from Sarnya 'cross yer new suspender bridge at the Falls, all the way up past Montreal to yer Riviera Loop de Loop. Of course yer "Grand Drunk" was jist an old nick's name. Full name was yer Great Western Sandwich and Winser R.R.***

But there was no railin' in any other part of the country (which wasn't called Canada yet). Yer new dubble province was Canada East and Canada West, and I guess east and west of *them* was jist called "out there." But by gol, there was a heckuva lotta "out

** Currant Feetnote: Still purty much the same today.

*** Inishul Feetnote: R.R. stands for Rural Root, since in them days ev'ry jerkwater got a stop.

91

there," and it was up fer grabs. If our fellas din't grab it, you know who would!

Us and U.S. had a bounder line, but that oney shows on a map. Sir Johnny he wanted a track on record that would be our missin' link-up. If anybody hadda ast Macdonald why this hole place of ours hadda be one country I don't s'pose he coulda told 'em. Anymore than that Headman Hillery when he clum Mount Everset twenty year ago with that sharper, Tent-sing. Johnny Macdonald woulda hadda give as his loco motive fer givin' birth to Canada same reason Hillery give fer havin' spiked his way to the top of that mountin': " 'Cause she's all there."

Yer Conflergration

It started with yer Charlatan's Confrence, that grate conflergration that was finely put out in 1867. Nobody much wanted it. Yer Marrytimers was up to their arms agin it when their leader Joseph "Seedy" How told 'em he was sellin' them up the river fer 80¢ a head.**

Yer Prince Edward Hylanders never joined up fer another six year, they was so puke-warm about it. My gol, yer Newfielanders kept *their* arms folded fer another eighty-two year, and some of 'em still got their fingers crost.

Yer Cuebeckers figgered it was another rip-off to be a minority grope with the rest of yer Anglish popilation. And that's what they called it, "Rip by Pop."

Even them Westministers in yer Big Ben's Common House next to the Queen's Privy din't seem to care two-pants about Canada. You take both yer Benjymin Disruly and yer Willy Ewart Gallstone*** they was too busy tryin' to git in on some of that Yerupeen Free Trade (known nowadays as yer Common Mark-up).

I think the thing what forced us to git together was probly yer U.S. sybil war, when yer South-end States succeeded from yer North. That was after George Brown's body got fired from Fort Sumpter.

There was a lotta talk among yer Yanks about startin' up an Underground Railroad under yer Deetroit River to open up a

** Mixed Feetnote: Valeda thinks yer Seedy How was another fella, that used to sit on King Mackenzie's cabinet durin' yer World War Eleven.

*** Persnal Feetnote: Part of me become named after him. Not his last part but his middlepart, Ewart — pernounced Yurt. Mind, it'd bin closer to the truth to be called Charles Gallstone Farquharson.

second front. But about the oney ones what tried to come acrost us was a buncha loose Irish Feenymin who evaded us at both ends of Lake Ontaryo ... yer Ford Eery and yer Pressedcot. They tried to raise up our I.R.E. but fergot that our little green men was mostly orange. So they flat-footed it back acrost yer boarder and probly ended up coppin' a job as one of New Yawk's Feeniest.

But the real spirits behind yer Conflegration was pervided by Sir Johnny "Red Label" Macdonald, so let's drink a helth to the new country and hope she'll soon be goin' thru the changes fer the better.

The wife she wants to put in a pome which was made up to celibate our 1967 tencenty-all and was give by her, electro-cutin' it herself. This here ode is not the first she has writ; Valeda's bin a long-time oder, recitin' at many consorts fer yer Sick and Tired of yer United Church.

Ode on You, O Canada

(as writ and recit by Valeda Drain Farquharson,
Parry Sound, Ontaryo, July 1st, 1967.)

What is Canada to you?
This land so strong and true.
What does it make you think of,
And why and where and how?
Whenever I think of my country,
It seems like a great big cow.
Yes, a Guernsey or a Holsteen,
Is that sich a foolish notion?
Lappin' its fill of the waters
Of our very own Pasifick Ocean.
Then chewin' its cud on the Prayerees,
Right over yer Kickin' Horse Pass

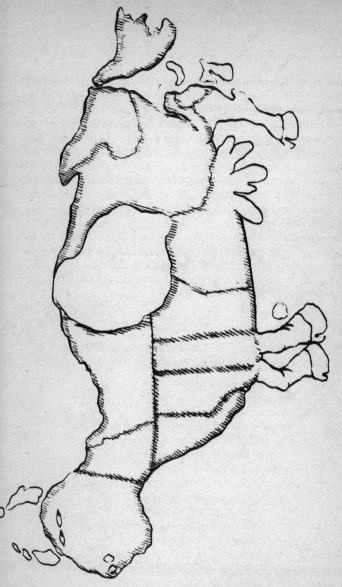

A fine upstandin' Holsteen country

In the breadbasket of our nation,
As it regurgitates its grass.
And settles its mash in Ontaryo,
Where its udders gently sway sweet,
Waitin' fer stockbrokers to milk it,
Down there on old Bay Street.
Then to the loins of our country,
Where somethin' surely is stirrin'!
Listen and you can hear
A rumblin' and grumblin' and whirrin'.
The wind of change is blowin'!
Can't you hear its howls?
As we wonder at all those movements
Deep in our nation's bowels.

And so we come to the end of my tail
And all its little rimes . . .
And doesn't this allus happen
To the dear old Marrytimes?

Yer Red River Serial (First Riel)

We was oney four provinces first off, but you take yer Sir Johnny Macdonald he was allus ready fer a fifth. He got worried about the soft underbelly of our breadbasket when a lotta Yanks started infilteratin' up our flanks and squattyin' on yer Winnypeg must-keg.

This was up in yer Norwester Terrytoryals where yer Hudson Bay was still a big facter. They din't seem to mind forners comin' up from yer south, but they warn't too keen on farmers comin' in from yer east. A lotta them farmers decided to git rid of yer Bay Boys and filed their partition up to Ottawa fer to have a big Hudson Bay Sale.

Upshat of it was a good deal was made of it on both sides. Yer Bay skint the guvermint fer a lotta money, and us farmers got another province, called then by an Irish name of yer Asinner-boyo. The oney ones left out on the deal was yer Injian and yer Matey, yer cold prayery's original residuents. Nobody bothered to tell them there was a new province where the deer and the antelope pay.

Them Matey Injians begun to hear a discurragin' word when surveyors started to pull the chain acrost their strip farms.** Turns out them plum-bobbers was surveyin' ahead of theirselves. Yer Hudson's Bayers had moved out, but Ottawa hadn't yet moved in, so ev'rybody was jist hooverin' around in a vackyume.

Up jumps a smart haff-brooder name of Louie Riel, starts to run the vackyume and clean up fer his own people. Louie he'd bin purty near a priest but jist missed takin' orders. Sure loved to give them tho'. He and his Mates took over the Fort Garry

---

** Pink Feetnote: Valeda din't want me to find out about that kinda Dukeabhor aggerculture. She says you don't have to be indecent to make a bare livin'.

Hotel and roust Guvner McDoogle outta his room and private bath.

Things started to happen. Bishop Sashay got recalled from the Vaticacan fer to try some of his divine intravention. Donald Smith was sent out with a bag of money by Ottawa but couldn't git a room at the Fort Garry 'cause they din't b'leeve it was his real name. He changed it to Lord Strathacorona and they even put up his horse.

But one fella, Tom Scot of the Orange Lodge, jist sassed Louie somethin' offal. Louie put him in the cooler but he kept gittin' hotter, so hot Scot got shot. Well sir, that sure started things off with a bang and we ain't heard the end of it yet. You could write off the next hundert years by the smoke from that one shell. Troops of Orangemen was sent out, Louie become a fidgetive from yer just sassiety, and a lot of his Mateys got knocked off.

That was the end of yer first Riel, and more to come. The reason give fer all them bullits was one fella was a Orangeman and the other was R.C. But my gol, that ain't what it was about atall. It was pullin' yer chain over another man's land without a buy-yer-leave. Any workin' man knows how that feels when the new highway or the new high-rise condominimum goes thru.

Them same scars is showin' more 'n ever today. I'm not talkin' 'bout Cuebec and yer War Measurers; I mean where my old people come from up there in Belfast. Them fellas is shootin' up each other jist 'cause the one is Orange and the other's Green, and that's got nothin' to do with the real reasons.

The real trubble with yer Londondairyer is yer Japs. It was them Yokohomo shipyards after the war learned how to bild the same boats we did cheaper and faster than us Ulcermen. That's all. You give a man work and enuff bread and he don't have to shoot at his naybors fer goin' to church.

If that Riel bullit had hit another Cathlick you might never have heard any more about it. But we did.

It's time we fergit about it tho' and git after yer high costa keepin' up livin', and yer inflammation, and yer thousands of unemployables, and never mind who goes to what Sundy Scool fer to play Bingo or anythin' else.

Off Yer Rail

Now that them Red Riverers was settled down and startin' to call each other Manytoberers, old Johnny Macdonald was thinkin' of stretchin' our bellyband again. By this time Birtish Clumbia was makin' sheepish eyes his way, mainly on accounta their last year's Gold Rush had peter out.

The town they'd bilt speshully fer minors had gone to the dogs (which is why it's now called Barkervill) and you even hadda watch yer step on that Carrypoo Trail. But yer B.C.'s was waitin' fer somethin' else with steam risin' from it to be comin' 'round yer mountin', and when she come, that's when they'd sign in as Number Six.

So Sir Johnny he set out to raise some capitolists. But to show them Victorians and New Westministers he wasn't foolin' he give a fella name Sendfer Phleming his walkin' papers fer to lay everythin' he could on a map, so's they'd be ready to start bildin' accordion his bluepoints.

It was easy to git started on paper, but harder to raise yer rail. Money that time was titer 'n a bull's arse in fly-time.** Some of the Grits thunk Sir Johnny shoulda riz up the money from yer public sextors 'stead of scratchin' around yer private. But due to yer Recent Prostity Treaty, yer tarf was already purty high on deported goods without addin' no Exercise Tacks.

But our John finely got a tite wadda money from a buncha Canuck sindycats had made their piles in the U.S. Turned out they'd made it railroadin' too. One sure way to git to be a malted millyonair in them days was to be in yer railroad supply bizness, then git yerself a contrack fer to bild an R.R. Then you'd sell

** Sore Feetnote: Valeda got madder 'n a set hen when I got this one out. She feels I shoulda used the plite word fer it, which is yer *animal*, not yer *bull*.

yerself all the stuff you said you needed at yer own price. It was better 'n gold-brickin' or counter-feetin'. Don't think yer guvermint M.P.'s din't git in on the racket too, formin' their own companies and sellin' track to you and me from their own backyards. Now that's what you'd call a public trussed.

Well, when he got the money, Sir John he started burnin' it at both ends. He had two track teams workin' each coast and layin' fer each other till they met in the middle. Accordin' to Phleming's map that shoulda bin about Moosejaw, but one of yer teams made a pass thru yer Yellahead thru yer Rocky and the other fellas got micksed up in yer Kickin' Horse's Ass and come out way below yer Moosejaw, about Moosenee.

When the neither of them met, they both kept on trackin' to the other end of yer country, and that's why today we got two railroads, yer C.N. and yer C.P.

But I'm gittin' ahead of myself, as Julius Seizure said when they showed him his bust. (Now there's another Mornin' Smile, even if Valeda don't laff.)

Them two sets of trackers had hardly took off their ties and got down to work when there was an offal stink in yer Common House lit by this specifick scandle. Turns out Johnny Macdonald had bin gittin' a little more grease from them big railroad wheels than we all knew about.

A vote was took. There was a lotta no confidence men agin him, him and his party was railroaded outta office and Sir Johnny's pet projeck was stop in its track. By the time them Grits put him thru their mill, he come out of it lookin' like the gratest Toree ever sold.

Yer Rail On

Well sir, after old Johnny Macdonald's chickens come home to the rooster, he slipped under the table to become Leader of yer Opposite Position. His place as Primer Minister was took over by Alex Sandy MacKinsey, who I s'pose was tired of discoverin' all over Canada by that time. You mind he was the Scotch fella never had a map, started out west fer Prince Rooper and ended up north in yer frosted-perm with yer hardenin' of yer Articks.**

It may be jist a co-hinky-dinky two fellas havin' the same slur-name; anyways this here Alex Sandy MacKinsey was a stoned Mason. As head of yer Common House he turned out to be a block offa the old chip. Fer four years he sat there stiff and stately, hardly movin' atall jist like yer av'rage statute. Meantime yer coastercoast railroad got rustier 'n the hinges on a old maid's hope chest.

And there was Sir Johnny left standin' in the roundhouse without a corner to hiss in. But he got his steam up next 'leck-shun, and was back on the old stumpin' grounds tellin' ev'rybody to exorcise their french-fries on his b-haff.

They done it too. Them Torees got back in quicker 'n a sailor on shore leave. And the first thing Sir John done was mount a few soldyers and start up yer R.C.M.P.'s.***

Seems a buncha Yanky bootyleggers had bin crossin' the boarder into Alberto and cheatin' our Injians outta their furs by givin' them bad licker. Ev'rybody was so sick of them rennygades

** Frozen Feetnote: Valeda don't think it was the same one, but two fellas with yer same name. She looked up the both of 'em in yer Dick-shunary of Natural Biograffiti and there they was, both names spelt the same as two pees in a pot.

*** Inishul Feetnote: Valeda says to 'splain that John never mounted yer Roamin Cathlick Members of Parlment, but yer musical riders.

doin' this, they called the place where they done it Fort Whoop-up. Well sir, it wasn't too long before our Mounted Redcaps got a half nelson eddy on them U.S. boozehounds. They skeedaddled acrost yer Mount Anna boarder and never showed theirselves up our way agin till they got back in bizness in yer 1920's when Warshinton legallyized Inhibition.**

Second thing on old Johnny Macdonald's list was makin' tracks fer the west coast with his C.P.R.R. He ast a Canadian who was livin' in the States, Big Jim Hill, to bild the hole rig fer him. Jim, he had haff an eye fer to do it, but he wanted to run his rails down thru yer Mid-Wester States so's it'd tie up with all his own branches comin' outta Toolooth and Millwalky. But old John knew it ain't too good to have to step in yer naybor's backyard ev'ry time you wanta use the shanty. He was a paterotic all-Canadian was our John, din't have too much truck with no-body but his own, even tho' he warn't born here. In fack he once said: "A Birtish subjeck I was bored, but a U.S. objeck, no sirree!"

So instead of gittin' a Canuck what lived in the States, Sir John hired hisself a Yank ended livin' up in Canada. His name was Van Horen and he was a ring-tailed snorter of a billy-goad. He smoked like a steaminjun, drank like a dubble boiler, and swore like a conductor with a hot box. But he was an offal driver, and he got the hole she-banger laid in haff the time she was to of took.

The oney trubble at yer Common House end was razin' all the cash. Old Sir Johnny was floating' lones and waterin' the stock till he was up to his armed-pits in sudsities. But he knew there was oney two things would hold this country together: à rail-road, and the fack that ev'rybody else hates Tronto. But purty

** Dry Feetnote: Valeda claims all that Inhibition was done mostly by the good work of yer W.C. to you.

soon it got to be a case of weather a railroad was goin' to run acrost yer hole country, or yer country was goin' to be run into yer hole in the ground.

This pit Sir John into a kinda deepression, as well as keepin' him on the horns of a dillenema. But he got offa his horns when Louie yer Riel come back from States-side where he'd bin spendin' his part time teachin' scool and his other part bein' inmated in a funnyhouse.**

Seems Louie was assed back here by his Mateys who was bothered by the railroad-bildin' which was makin' it hard fer them to cross over the tracks and hunt up their Buffalo connections. So they had joined up with the Big Three of yer Injian Cheefs — Big Bare, Crowsfeet, and Poundcaker.***

Well sir, if it was yer railroad started this haff-brood trubble, it was yer railroad finished it in short orders. Sir John was able to rush troops under General Middleman flat in no time by rails. They carried him out hard by Saskytune with his rattlin' Gat gun, but mind you, even with all that he never done too good agin yer Matey leader, Gabe Dupont.

Gabe he was a man of a few words, mainly on accounta he never learned to read nor wrote, but my gol, you stand him on the next concession and he could shoot the tips offa yer bull. Him and his little buncha Matey irregular gorillas purty near beat the retreat offa all them Reglar Army Malicious.

But God he's on the side of yer Big-B Eyetalians, as the Pope can tell you. It warn't too long before them poor Mateys was surrounded up, Gabe Dupont lit out fer the States and ended up as a sharkshooter with Annie Oakvill in Wild Billy Hitchy-

---

** Twisted Feetnote: Valeda says from what she's heard about yer Yank scoolin', it was probly the other way 'round.

*** Crows Feetnote: Crowsfeet he finely pulled out 'cause he din't like the new wrinkle they was plannin' to pull, namely yer White Massa Cree.

cock's Three-Ring Bulls-eye Show. As fer the Riel leader, Louie got arrested in his development and tried fer sev'ral treasons. They finely tied the knot on him** nine days after yer last spike was driv up Craig's Alley-key to finish off yer C.P.R.

The main thing to 'member is that since that time our Injians and Mateys haven't give us no real trubble. And that's the way it's gonna have to be if we're not gonna have any of that inter-rachel trubble up here in Canada. Myself, I think we're gonna have piece, jist as sure as shootin'.

** Knotty Feetnote: Some Orange people claims he was jist as well hung. Valeda says it don't matter what they did to him, you can't call it tyin' the knot which oney refers to yer state of holy acrimony. Myself I think she's out of it, fer nowadays when a young couple talks about tyin' their knot, they're more 'n likely talkin' about yer Vasextummy.

This finish off of yer C.P.R. is from a derogatory type took by an old brownie of the time

Yer Poet, Lorry, eh?

When Sir Johnny Macdonald finely passed on to yer Great Conservatory-in-the-Sky, his place was took by a purty old man, Mackenzees Bowel, who found trubble gittin' people innerested in any of the movements he placed on the floor of yer House.

So come next election, yer Tories was out, and we was handed a brand new bag of Grits under a fella had a silver tongue to match his long lox. You mind Sir Wilful Lorry, eh? He sure cut a poetical figger, in his candyfloss hair and his frog-tailed coat. When he went over fer yer old Queen of Victoria's dymond-jewbilly, he struck her so fancy she ast to have him nightied.

Mind you, he was pretty frale in health ever since he become leader, when the mantle fell on him at a grate Libral party. But don't let that fool you, fer beneath that velvet coat there was a iron ham in it, and he could act like a reg'lar automat.

One of the things he went right to work and done, was to settle up yer West. Ever since yer second Riel fit had been fot, most folks was scared to live out there fer fear of gittin' tommy-hocks in their backyard. But Sir Wilf he told his Minister fer Yer Inteerier to put adds in the newspapers all over yer world, advertizin' "The West, A Nest, and Ewe." And by gol, if a lotta sheepish farmers din't turn up from as far-away as yer Ukerain, some Dukeabhors from behind yer Rurals, and they even got a herd of Crotes by the Balkin's. Before too long, ev'rybody was bustin' their sods to set up a homin'stead, and before you could say Jack Pickerelsgill we had us two new Prayery provi-dences.

Another thing Wilf done was to set up yer Penny Post Office under yer General Pastmaster, Sir Willyam Mulehock. Right away it got to be more poplar than "Snakes 'n Ladders." Before Christmas they hadda dubble their staff in Ottawa. Yessir, hadda have the two of 'em there, one fer settin' and sortin', the other fer standin' and handin'.

One thing Sir Wilf got mixed up in he mebbe wisht he hadn'ta was yer Boor War. This hole thing started when some of yer bigger Boors refused to let an Anglishwoman, Lady Smith, use one of their public conveenyances which was sedgeregated on accounta in yer South of Afrike they don't use nothin' but yer apart-heads. Well sir, it took an offal lotta troops from all over yer Umpire to make sure that Lady Smith got releeved, and before it was all over some of our boys had a hand in it.

Wilf also give Canada its first navy, called yer "Tinpot Navy," meanin' it really wasn't much. Yer Canadian Admirables was all give shore duty at yer Royl Navel Hospitable where they was aloud to be in charge of all yer vessles on the third floor. Wilf got in trubble from all sides fer this. Yer Cuebeckers thought he was actin' too Anglish, and the rest of us thought he was regurgitatin' back to bein' a darn fool Frenchman. Ackshully, it was a case of six of one and a haff a case of the other, but this same sorta thing happens today if you read the handwritin' on yer Common House wall.**

Lookin' back on his speeches, there was one other thing Sir Wilf was wrong about. He's the one what said: "Yer Twentieth-Century belongs to Canada." I think if you'll check the books, 'speshully the bankbooks, you'll find out yer Twentieth-Century still belongs to Fox (whoever he is).***

** Dirty Feetnote: Valeda won't let me print any of that stuff here. I told her there was nothin' obsolene, but since she can't check on it fer herself you'll have to take my words fer it.

*** Filmy Feetnote: Valeda she's more parshul to yer Paramour Pitchers, them as made yer greatest Love Story ever tole.

Yer Kyzer Rolls

King Edward yer Seven was the first outta Victoria by Albert,
so he sat on his mother's throne when she got finished. He soon
become known as yer "Playboy King" with the big centre spread.
He finely got laid by yer West Minister's Abby and all of the
kings of Yerup come to his last confinement. There was Kyzer
Billy of Germny, yer Zar Nickelass of Roosia, and Fran's Josef,
yer Impurer of Australia-Hungry.

Funny thing was that all them fellas was kissin' cuzzins,
and jist four years later they was all Grate Warrin' with each
other. And I don't mean jist a fambly drunk-up on a Sardy
night; I mean a more 'n four year bash what got the hole
world in a mess.

I'm not too sure what started the hole thing off; I think
Fran's Josef got his hair assassinated somewheres in Suburbia.
But Kyzer Billy-B.Dam was jist itchin' fer a fight anyways, him
and his Chief Staff and Comfort, Vaughan Hinderburger, better
known as "old blood and guts."**

The reason them high mucky-mucks in Yerup got into conflick was 'cause they was allus playin' alleys. Yer French was
alleyed up with yer Roosians, and yer Germins was tradin' dibs
with yer Oster-Hunkies. But come 1914, these boys was playin'
fer keeps.

Now you'll wonder how Canada got drug into all of this, but
at that time she done whatever yer Birtish said, and accordin'

** Raised Feetnote: Valeda hasn't heard sich langridge since she last
went down with me to yer Packers. I go down reg'lar with a loada Tam-
worths or Poland Chinas and come back aloan, but it's nicer to have
company both ways.

to some kinda Boner Law yer Birtish was alleys with little Bellygum.**

So when yer Kyzer rolled acrost Bellygum, that set Canada right up beside the alleys, which meant our best young men hadda go off by theirselves fer four years. Most of our country thought it was a paterotic thing to do, but there was two bunches din't agree. One was yer French Canucks and the other was yer farmer all over. They both wanted the young fellas to stay at home and git in the hay. I can't say as I blame them, fer this hole World War Part One shoulda never took place. If all us workin' people had mebbe struck out and lay down on the job, them crowned potentaters of Yerup mighta hadda do the fightin' theirselves. You can bet there'da bin no contest.

Mind you, once our boys was in, they sure felt their presents. They extinguished themselves at places like Eep, Passiondale, and Shimmy Ridge. Some of 'em was even up in the air with yer Royl Flyin' Corpse. One of these boys, a bishop from Owen Sound, shot the aces offa seventy-two Jerries over yer Red Barrens.

A lotta our rejmints come outta that war covered in, 'sides other things, glory. Their names are Legion, and you'll probly find them at the back of the hall. But to name jist a few, there was yer Tronto Scotties, yer Princess Patties, yer Vin Douce (they was a Cuebec rejmint used to carry sweet wine in their water bottles), and them Montreal Ladees from Hadees, yer Black Watches. I guess yer Germin calvary had never seen fellas draggin' acrost nomads land in skirts before, and when they shouted their war cry, "Dior Go Bra," them Jerry horses jist

** Corrective Feetnote: Valeda don't think we spelt it right, but anyways it's the little place that hard between yer Flander Feeled and yer Holland Marsh.

112

reared up and all you could see was a clouda horeshat and small stones.**

Well, it's all over now, and ev'ry November 11, we shut up fer two minutes jist to perpetuate yer Grate War and buy a poppy fer them as dyed in vein. But by gol, if that was the war to end wars we coulda done without it, includin' yer Treat of Versehigh and yer Leega Nation.

Twenty year later, the hole rang-dang-doo come up agin, and agin our best young fellas left their bones bleachin' behind them. Valeda thinks the next war should be fought in Absentya . . . wherever that is.

** Bare Teatnote: Valeda says "Dior Go Bra" is the same thing shouted today by yer Women's Librium when they burn off their chest supports. Well, yer Black Watches never done that, but knowin' the way they dress, I figger they musta burned their britches behind them.

Yer Next to Last Post

When yer post war finely come, we was all under Sir Robert Boredem and his Coal-Issue guvermint. Sir Robert he give over the seals in his office to Arthur Me-in, 'cause he wanted to retire with his wife Elsie, yer Lady Boredem.

But it was time fer the country to go to the poles, and when yer returns was in, Me-in was out. It was a new start-up name of King Mackenzie assended his way to power. And he staid there fer the next three decadents, give or take an R.B. Benny.

One reason we had a King so long was, he was the oney man in Canada had the trick of sittin' on the fence and at the same time keepin' his ear to the ground. He warn't a tall man neither, altho' that statute they put to him outside yer Common House must be purty near nine feet tall, but you know how them Grits tend to eggs-aggregate.

Durin' yer War, King he'd bin down in yer States in labor, which is mebbe why he wasn't prescripted fer the Army. He come back here to be a sybil servant but finely got elected into his office after bein' ejected a coupla times and even once blowin' his deposit. But once he was in, he staid in, like Flinn.**

When it come to gittin' down to bizness King he b'leeved more 'n less in yer *lazy fairy*.*** But a buncha Westerners was gittin' tired of bein' the sandwich 'tween yer Eastern profitears and yer Ottawa frate rates. So they got up a party

---

** Dashin' Feetnote: Valeda wanted to know who Flinn was, but when I told her it was yer moovy man, she minded him as the Errall Flinn used to swash his buckle a lot. She watched him take off his part in yer title roll when Queen Elizabetty Davis was drivin' that old Essex.

*** By-lingamal Feetnote: This jist means "keep yer hands offa my bizness."

114

of their own and call it One Big Union. This never caught on much back East, partly 'cause in French it comes out like Une Beeg Onion, and the other partly 'cause yer Ontaryo farmer was already united in yer U.F.O. which had nothin' to do with yer unindemnifiable flying objecks.**

Some mettle workers in Winnypeg went even further out. They'd heard about yer Roosian Evolution got up by yer Marks Brothers, Tropsy, and Lemin, and they figgered they could try the same kinda Bullshyvism at yer Porridge and Main. All they did was sit on their rights fer a six week general strike-out, but the way them Mounties rid their horses agin them, you'da thought they had decomposed King Mackenzie and had him abdicatered. I know yer R.C.M.P.'s allus gits their man, but did they have to go after their women and childern too?***

But none of this uprest ever got nowheres. That sly little King, he jist smiled like a Chesthire Cat and talked a lotta garbiage till nobody knew where they was at, 'cept him, who was still in. I think the oney time anybody ever heard that man commit hisself out loud was the time he patted his dog and said: "It's a bitch."

One good thing that happen durin' his rain about this time was at yer Best-Banty Instantoot where they found out you don't have to die a suger-beetis if you have enuff Insolence. Them fellas got the Noble Prize fer this, and Valeda's kinda sorry they din't git medals from Parry Sound and Mactier as well.

Another bit of culture that come up was yer Grope of Seven — a buncha drawers clustered together and went around the

** Hushed-puppy Feetnote: And nothin' to do with what uno-who said under his breath in Parlymint.

*** Red Feetnote: Valeda don't think it was our Mounties coulda shoved them people around. Mebbe it was the horse's asses under 'em.

north country paintin' barns and outbildin's by the numbers.

But fer my kinds of culture —yer horti and yer agri — it was yer boom and yer bust. Wheat'd be two dollars yer bushel one year and a dollar fer two the next. All yer av'rage farmer'd git fer his sweat haff the time was a little Pool of Wheat. But then in yer mid-Twenties, yer boom stuck fer years and ev'ry-body figgered posterity was around the corner. Yer Farmers' Movements petered theirselves out, and about the oney thing really lasted was the women gittin' over their suffrage and able to vote. Mind you, the girls is oney jist now comin' to the point of standin' up in the Men's Rooms fer their rights.

But rights or lefts, it din't matter in '29 when them broker fellas on Wall Street told us all their bottoms had fell out.

Yer Dip Depressyun

Yer Big Crash on yer un-Live Stock Market sure put a crimp in the 1930's meetin's of our Parry Sound Progress Club. There was even talk of turnin' yer Pomp-payin' Room of our Brunswick Hotel into a soup kitchen. Many a man 'round our concession was pullin' outta his small-holder fer to move down to Tronto and join them urbane unemployables on the Pogey.

But us mixed-up farmers had a better time of it than them one-a-croppers out West. Wheat was gittin' 38¢ the bushel, but thru yer lien years of yer drout hardly no crap atall was up-comin'. Fer five year — that'd be yer '33 to '37 — yer hole West was dryer'n a bird's is in August. When yer rain did come finely, it come down solid, and all them poor Westerers could croak was: "Gang, Gang! The hail's all here!"

Yer choice wheats that year was yer No. 1 Rusty and yer No. 2 Smutty. You'd think Ottawa woulda tried to help ev'rybody, but there was a lotta conflick 'tween yer Pervincials and yer Dumbminions. King Mackenzie he sat on his fence and said he'd be gosh-darned if he'd give a nickel to any outta-workers under a Tory Pervincial Premeer. Well, after he said that, I wouldn'a give a nickel fer his chances in the 'lection. And sure as hootin' yer R.B. Benny fit in and King was out with his dumb minions.

Now it's hard to say whether we all voted fer R.B. yer Sundy Scool teacher or R.B. yer millyonair lawyer.** Myself I think it was yer comby-nations of yer both, most people bein' curious as to how a fella could be the two things at once.

R.B. figgered if he couldn't raise the wheat, the least he could

** Dry-rot Feetnote: Valeda thinks I should start callin' myself C.F.R.B. Farquharson, bein' as how I'm quallyfied fer Crop Failure, Retired Bankrupt.

do was raise the tarfs. I think on that one he shoulda checked with yer exports. There was nothin' goin' outta the country and nothin' comin' in. Yer bizness cycles was in yer state of suspended constipation. A buncha unemployds out on yer West Coast tried to steal a march on Ottawa, but oney got as far as Regina where they was met with many-fistos pervided by yer R.C.M.P. The big Boy Scouters was still out to git their man even if he din't have a job.

Up to that time we was all in Canada either Toree or Grit. But people out West had got so fed up with not bein' fed, they up and went on parties of their own. Yer C.C.M. was a veehickle thunk up by yer well-known five-and-dimer, J.S. Woolworth. And yer Sociable Crediters was drummed up by Bible Billy A.B. Hart. He was one of yer Prayery Evangels was allus seein' pie in the sky, and promisin' ev'rybody a cut.

Down-and-out Cuebeckers wanted to have a party, and Morris Duplenish was jist the fella to give it to 'em. He give it to 'em good fer twenty year, but not so good as he took, which was Duplenty. So much that he finely hadda pass a Padlock Law fer his piggy bank.

The Depressyun was hardly felt by yer Marrytimes 'cause they thought it was s'posed to be like that. But out in Newfieland they hadda be baled out by Grate Breton. She took over the hole island in '33 — hook, line, and sunker. And people was so depressed there was nary a sound of protest, 'cept fer the odd Screech.

Mind you, ten year later Newfieland was a-boomin'! And so was yer Western panhandlers! Why? 'Cause yer war guns was a-boomin' too. Seems like ev'rytime they stop makin' a killin' on yer Stock Market and go into a Dip Depressyun, the oney way they git out of it is by makin' a killin' on each other. No wonder yer Homely Sapio is soon gonna make hisself an ex-stink.

Yer Second Whirl at War

You take yer av'rage war, it's an offal price to pay fer gittin' outen a bizness slump and into yer holycost. There warn't so many uniform fellas knocked off as yer '14-'18 ruckus, but a turble lotta plainclothes people. Fifty millyun. This kinda post-naval berth control is cuttin' off yer nose to spike yer drink.

How it started was yer Germin, yer Eyetalian, and yer Jap all had Axes 'tween them. Yer Germin started first, stuck his nose into Pole-land. The first six months or so was called yer "phoney war," 'cause nothin' really happened; both sides was jist phonin' it in behind their lines. Yer French was behind their Maggynose Line, and as fer yer Germin, well you must remember us all singin' "We're gonna hang out Warshin'ton yer Ziegfeld line."

But all that stopped when Germins bliss-creaked their way into our Netherglands. After that yer Eyetalian dick-tater Muscle Eeny stabbed someone's back in France, and yer Axes was in.

Yer Birtish hadda evaccinate theirselves hard by Dumcurk, and Bungle fer Breton. That's when Never Chamberlinen folded like his umbrella. In come Winsome Church-hill to give us yer two fingers up and told yer Naztys to bring on their Pansy Divisions. But my gol, they never come. Twenty miles of Chanel and they never set a goosed foot on yer White Cleft Dover.

Her man Goring thought he'd conker by airmales. He ordered yer Berlitz on London and his Lustwafflers kept droppin' bums over St. Pall's and other sites fer sore eyes. But when we sent up a few Spittlefires, them Germin Junkies went scurvyin' back to their Fodderland.**

** Flyin' Feetnote: Valeda says how could them Germins teach Junkies fer to fly. I told her it was the names of their airplanes, and now she won't let me mention them other Fokkers and Messyschitz.

Well sir, after yer Big Berlitz come yer Long Sitz. Ev'rybody sat around on the end of their Lendleash.

Next thing happen was way out in yer High-wayin' Islands hard by Honeylooloo, when a buncha Bananzy Jap pilots committed Mata Harry on yer U.S. Navel. This was a dirty trick and so was what we done to our–Canadian Japs right after. Our Japs was mostly all Vancoover-born, never seen yer Nip-on. Jist the same, they was round-up, confiscated of their homes, and sent deep into Canada to be inturd.

Now this ain't histry to me. I 'member it at the time. I was by now one of yer Privates in yer Royl Muskoka Dismounted Foot. We started in yer bull-pen at yer Colossalinoleum in Tronto, moved to Camp Boredem, and on to Petaweewee. I felt like one of yer Kellogg Reg'lars 'cause I was allus on the go. I finely ended up at yer Hamilton Trades Scool as a Second Class Artifice. I spent mosta my leaves in London, Paris, and Brantford.

I never got over-seized tho'. I got the Spam Medal without yer Armor Star, but b'leeve me, I'da gone ... with all them Seagram Hylanders and Guvner General's Mudguards. ... I wasn't one of them Zombies fightin' King to stay in our Country.

Now you mind in yer First Whirl of War, I synthesized with yer insolationists. But not this time, no sirree Bob, and I'll tell you why. This time it wasn't no Kyzer itchin' fer a fight fer want of nothin' better to do. This time it was that Nazty cyclepath, Hitler, was wantin' to put the kybosh on a hole buncha people ... namely yer Jew. Now before I joined up I don't think I'd met more'n one Jew in my life. He was a little truck-drivin' sheeny name of Lipman, used to by chickens offa me mebbe twice a month fer cash. He never tried to jew me down and I never tried to gentle him up. It was just bizness doin' bizness with him ... cut and dry ... but allus above yer board.

And it made me mad to think that Hymie Himmler and his S.S. Gepasto was tryin' to send the likes of Lipman and his fambly to camp fer the summer where none of 'em wouldn't git back.

We hadda lotta French fellas from Cuebec couldn't see goin' over to fight when yer prescription finely come out. They din't wanta fight somebody else's battles, and fer that I don't blame 'em. But yer Airy-huns — yer Goring and yer Goballs — was after the hole rang-dang-doo of us fer to be slaves fer their Massa Rates. And we'd all have to be "stricken-yer-Doytch" and mebbe after a time git wiped right outta yer race. That'd be yer Jenny-side.

Now yer Cuebecwas (as yer Seprator calls hisself) fellas today is worried 'bout the same thing; mebbe some of 'em understand better now what that war was all about.

Agin Yer Post

I guess you all know who won that Number Two War we had. It was yer Germin and yer Jap, and don't stop to give me an argymint. Yer libel to git run over by a Folksywagon or a Toyola Coronary.

But back in '45 we all thought that we'd won it ('cept fer them as cellybrated yer D-J Day in Hallyfacks, where it looked more like yer start of Number Three).

Despike that, yer post times was lookin' good. There'd bin a bit of a gap in yer generators, but now our Armed Forcers was comin' home to have childern of their own fer a change. Purty soon the guvermint was eggin' them on by handin' out Baby Boners, which is one way of makin' allowance fer the fambly. Them as had no childern to speak of could list them at yer Apartment fer Veteran's Affairs.

Ev'rythin' else was bustin' and boomin' too. Out Edmundton way they was gittin' oil by lickin' the tar outen the sands; over in Labbydoor they was ironin' out the ground (mostly fianced by yer Yanky oarmasters); down in Sarnya they was comin' up with sympathetic rubbers; and Gagger Counters up by Grate Bare Lake was lookin' up Uranyum.

A lotta immigrance come out to swell up our berth rate, and the first off was yer Newflounderers. After all them years they finely joined up with us when they got a talkin' to by their Small Wood head.

We boomed fer five year, then started to sputter, coff, and spit out chaff. It was yer U.S. Martial Plan with their Forrinade dispenser done it. They was subsistin' their own farmers so's they could ship wheat to yer Auntie Commonest fer the Good Will. That left us grain-groars up here holdin' our full bag.

We had grain comin' outen our elevators till we hadda spill our seed on the ground, like that fella in the Bible.**

Funny enuff in them sirplus years, our one good customer was yer Serviet Union, mainly on accounta yer Yank had already opened a Cold Wore with them. Now, of course, we're sellin' to yer Chinee, but back then they split down the middle 'tween yer Shank-high Czechs and yer Matzy Tongue.***

Things got a little hostel with yer Kareer War. It's s'posed to have started when yer North Kareerists invaladed yer South acrost yer Thirty-eighth Parrylell bars. (That's what they say about yer Veep Congs too, them gorillas in yer black peejamas.)

Anyways, trubble allus seems to break out jist when there's a slump in yer airyframe industry down by Callyfornia where all the lemons comes from. Seems like there's nothin' like a good little war to pick up yer spare parts and git them flyin' agin. Oney trubble is, spare partsa people start flyin' 'round too. Right now we're all neuter so far as yer Veet Napalm's concerned — jist makin' profits sellin' the hardware.

But back in yer Kareer, we was into sev'ral thousand of our fellas servin' yer Unightied Nations. And some of 'em got to be prisoners too, but thanks to yer Red Crossers they allus got their parsels ev'ry month and their brains washed ev'ry Sardy night.

Back home, one of our big steps was gittin' a local boy the job of Guvermint-Genral. Vince Messey of yer McCormick an' Dearin' outfit broke in the job purty good. He later got permoted and moved to yer U.S. to be over Young Doctor Killjoy on the

** Old Testy Feetnote: That'd be yer Onan, but our boy Orville clames it warn't his falt since he suffered from yer Port Noise Complaint.

*** Yella Feetnote: I'm bound to say yer Chineeman was split that way, but I'm not too sure about his woman — havin' heard roomers on the side.

T.V. But he left us his Messey Report which made us buy-culture-all.

First thing was yer Rank moovy man, Alix Gwinnest come over to Stratfurd-on-Taryo fer to take off Richard's Third Part. And he done it good fer a fella with the arthuritis offal bad. They called this rang-dang-doo yer Shakespeer Festerall, but you'd think they woulda got it up in Shakespeer-on-Taryo 'stead of makin' ev'rybody go six miles all the way into Stratfurd fer to see it.**

'Round this time yer 'Merkens started comin' up here to stare at our assets. They thought Canada was a natural gas and wanted to take it home with 'em. Old Seedy How, he was gonna let them, had ev'rythin' rigged up fer the sell-out and tried to closure Common House so's there'd be no rebate. Well sir, he was figgerin' without Long John Doofenbeaker, who wouldn't be shut up and hasn't since. John started yer long-windiest gabbin' match ever seen in Canada when he pulled out his fill-yer-buster. The Guvermint called it yer Pipe-Down Rebate, but John he talked his way acrost the floor from yer Opposite Position to yer Premeer's ship.

Valeda and I both voted fer him, but then we bin Retrogressive Preservatives ever since her Great-Grandpa Boyle lost the Post Office when Sir Wilful DuMaurier blew in.*** I know Doofenbeaker done good things like yer Billy Rites, but the

** Blank Feetnote: Valeda was down once fer to feed yer swans and see that "Roll Me Over, Juliette." She says the hole thing was a fake. It was some skinny, dark-haired girl, not atall our pet, Juliette. And she never sang one song, jist said "G' night, Mom," stabbed herself, and dropt dead.

*** Fambly-Tree Forked Feetnote: That'd be yer Great-Grampa Boyle on the mother's side. Valeda she's a Boyle on her mother's side and a Drain on her father's.

oney thing stand out fer me was the times that Gertie Mudslinger presented her briefs to yer Cabinet.

It was Leslie Piercin', one of yer Middle-Easter diplomatterers, took over from the "Prints Albert Profit." First thing he done was to let the old flag fall and let the Union Jack off.**

The oney thing I 'member about Piercin's Common House time was that stately Secretary Hedy LaMarsh runnin' 'round in a blonde rig and a minnie-mouse skirt shorter 'n a second crop of timothy. And, of course, there was yer big Exposé. But that was mostly done by yer French mare, Jean Dropout, to cellybrate yer old Conflergration and the openin' of his new restrunt.

But Valeda says it was yer Piercin' ayes brung about yer Seeway — all that clearin' land and bildin' lox down by Block-vill and Cornall so's we could see way acrost to yer other 'side what the Yanks was up to next. But I b'leeve she's wrong about that, fer it's called yer St. Lorrent Seeway, and that'd be the work of yer previous encumbrance, Louise St. Lorrent. Any-ways, Leslie Piercin' quit soon after yer Exposé to write a book about Hedy LaMarsh called, *I'm The Oney Gilty Bird in the Cage.*

His SusSex Drive place was took over by Premiere Trousseau, which means "first weddin' dress," but that din't happen till he was almost over yer Parlmint Hill. Valeda she voted fer him in '68. She thought Peeair looked so darn cute in his bear feat, scandals, and his asscot around his neck. But she's not gonna vote fer him next time, not after he aloud all them homo-sectionals to have free abortives.

Right now she's thinkin' it over. Myself I think it's a toss-off 'tween Yessirree-Bob Stansfeeled offerin' to lead us outta yer

** Sore Feetnote: Valeda still thinks our flag looks like we was all runnin' a Soopertest Gas Station.

Harvey Woods, and that Socialite Davey Loose who keeps pointin' his finger at yer Corpulent Bum. Mind you, there's plenty of farmers in Cuebec that will go for Real Cow-ette, yer Sociable Credit Card.

But, as yer Seprator Reeny Laveck would say, "I'm gittin' outta my province." Histry's what's already happen, and at this here writin' yer outcome is still futuristic and doubtful. So's our hole country's fer that matter, which brings me to . . .

Yer After-Word

This book was writ when it was too wet to plow and finished 'cause we had sich a rotten summer. Valeda thinks they should make a moovy this winter and call it yer "Summer of '72."

But the rain'll soon start to let up, so soon's I finish this little assay I'll be out on my Allis tryin' to finish the fallow. And I'll be heavin' my pre-Crambian stones fulla schist outen the way agin. That'll be histry makin' me repeat myself, and I know them rocks underfoot is gonna have the last laff on me when I'm under 'em.

You know what they say, "Never mind histry, it'll all be the same in a hundert year." But by gol, I keep wonderin' about the next five'r ten year. Them stones'll still be here and I might be too. But what about our hole country? That's what ev'rybody's askin', and more'n a few are layin' bets agin it.

Next month we got some Farquharson people comin' out from yer incestral home in Ireland. They're tickled to come, sick of all that syblin' warrin' with nary a sybil word 'tween naybors. They're gonna settle Aylmer Cuebec way where homes is cheaper. But will they be comin' out to the same thing agin?

Seems ev'rybody and his brother is tryin' to seprate. Even yer Women's Librium got spokesmen say they kin go it alone . . . don't need no help fer yer auto-eroticks.** Yer young people seprated from their parents long ago. Myself I can't hardly understand a thing our Orville says no more, and his hair has growed so long till he looks like a tired housekeeper. It makes me laff sometimes and swear others, but my gol, jist 'cause he has a langridge barryer don't make me wanta kick him outen the house.

** Twisted Feetnote: Valeda took that down as she was writ. She says she thinks that's what Orville's talkin' about when he wants to borry the pick-up fer to go to the Drive-In.

I think I know part of what them Seprators feels, fer if ever there was a first-rate second-class cityzen these days, it's yer small farmer. Sometimes when Bob Loblaws give me a price fer our aigs that don't make it worthwhile even cleanin' them off, I feel like sepratin' myself. Valeda she's allus at me to git down to yer assfalt jungle and live in them one-room high-rises that's so dinky ev'rytime you cross yer legs you kicks yer wife. But I'll stay on the farm, where you can fight with yer wife without bein' herd.

I used to worry 'bout us bein' yer Fifty-first State, but now I think all of 'em is granually movin' up here. I think they're gonna secede by us not really tryin'. But them Yanks aren't dumb. They know we got somethin' u-neek up here. Valeda's allus sayin' yer Yanks has no culture and yer Birtish has too much, and that's us in the middle — smug as a bug. Myself I like the idee of havin' *flocons de mais* fer breakfast, and bein' differnt and seprate from yer Birtish and yer Yanks . . .

Oh my gol, there's that word agin! Mebbe there's nothin' I can do 'bout it, but it'll be a goldarn shame if this country's national antrum is gonna be "Divide It, We Stand; Unite It, We Fall."

That's Yer End.

Yer Indecks

PaperJacks

PaperJacks, the paperback division of General Publishing Co. Ltd. (one of the few Canadian book companies owned by Canadians), is the most exciting and innovative mass market paperback program in Canada. It is designed to introduce in paperback books formerly published in hard cover as well as original works by Canadian authors. PaperJacks includes in its list such noted writers as Robert Thomas Allen, Tom Ardies, Margaret Atwood, John Ballem, Clark Blaise, Harry J. Boyle, Max Braithwaite, Barry Broadfoot, Sheila Burnford, Marian Engel, The Four Horsemen, Mavis Gallant, Anne Hébert, David Helwig, Harold Horwood, Donald Jack, Pauline Johnson, Thomas P. Kelley, John Latimer, Norman Levine, Nicholas Monsarrat, John Metcalf, Brian Moore, Martin Myers, Eric Nicol, Mordecai Richler, Marion Rippon, Charles Templeton and Richard Wright.

Since its inception PaperJacks has set industry-wide precedents, and will continue to provide good mass market books by important Canadian authors—books needed by Canadians at prices they can afford.